Racial Equality in America

The 1976 Jefferson Lecture in the Humanities

Presented by the National Endowment for the Humanities

Also by John Hope Franklin

The Free Negro in North Carolina, 1790–1860

From Slavery to Freedom: A History of Negro Americans

The Militant South, 1800–1860

Reconstruction after the Civil War

The Emancipation Proclamation

Land of the Free
with John Caughey and Ernest May

Illustrated History of Black Americans
with the editors of Time-Life Books

A Southern Odyssey: Travelers in the Antebellum North

John Hope Franklin

Racial Equality in America

The University of Chicago Press
Chicago and London

The University of Chicago Press, Chicago 60637
The University of Chicago Press, Ltd., London

81 80 79 78 77 76   987654321

Library of Congress Cataloging in Publication Data

Franklin, John Hope, 1915–
  Racial equality in America.

  (Jefferson lecture in the humanities; 1976)
  Bibliography: p.
  1. Afro-Americans—History—Addresses, essays,
lectures.   2. Afro-Americans—Civil rights—Addresses,
essays, lectures.   I. Title.   II. Series.
E185.F72   973'.04'96073   76–26168
ISBN 0–226–26073–9

To all those who believe in
and work for
racial equality in America

Contents

Preface

Shortly after the National Endowment for the Humanities invited me to be the Jefferson Lecturer for 1976 I decided to give the lecture in three parts in three different cities on "Racial Equality in America." The lecture was set in a historical framework, and the first part dealt with the problem of racial equality in Revolutionary America. Thomas Jefferson, as the author of the Declaration of Independence and of the highly significant *Notes on Virginia* and a leading thinker on social and political problems, was inevitably a central figure in any discussion of the subject. My choice of subject required an extensive examination of his racial views. That the lectureship was named in his honor had no bearing on my selection of a subject or on my treatment of it. And the content of the lecture was not influenced by the fact that it was the Jefferson Lecture. It was the lectureship, not the content of the lecture, that honored him.

In this lecture, I have addressed the problem of racial equality as Americans have confronted that problem since the seventeenth century. I have been concerned primarily with the equality of treatment and of opportunity, and I have given considerable attention to the denial of such equal treatment, especially as Negro Americans have experienced such denial through the years. The lecture has not had as its central concern the amelioration of conditions among blacks, for such actions, however praiseworthy, are reminiscent of the practice of humanizing the slave code during the antebellum years. As long as the context was one in which law or rigid customs and practices placed strict limitations on the nature and extent of amelioration, it was impossible for blacks to enjoy racial equality.

Equality, as used here, is not only an ancient concept whose roots go back to the Greek republics. It is also a concept deeply embedded in American constitutional law. One either has it or does not have it. Thus, it is scarcely germane to the central point to observe that blacks are better off now than they were a half-century ago or that they are better off here than they are in Zambia or Mauretania. The criterion by which to measure the status of their equality is neither 1926 nor some far-off principality. Rather, it is the status of their equality as set forth in the Constitution under which they live and the equality enjoyed by others who live under that same Constitution.

I have tried to adhere to the historian's role of describing and analyzing racial inequality in its historical setting. I made no attempt to chart the course for the achievement of equality in the future. As one reads the lecture, however, one may draw some lessons from past experiences and make some inferences regarding the most successful approaches—

and the least successful—in the effort to attain racial equality. In that way, what I have said may well be instructive. But the first objective was to provide some historical perspective without which no adequate guidelines to the future can be made in any case.

The sources of the poems quoted in this lecture are as follows: At the end of Part One, Langston Hughes, *The Langston Hughes Reader* (New York: George Braziller, 1958); at the end of Part Two, Countee Cullen, *Copper Sun* (New York: Harper and Brothers, 1927); in the text of Part Three, Witter Bynner, *Take Away the Darkness* (New York: Alfred A. Knopf, 1947), and at the end of Part Three, by A. W. Thomas, quoted in W. E. B. Du Bois, *Black Reconstruction* (New York: Harcourt, Brace, 1935). I am grateful to the authors and publishers concerned.

Dr. Ronald Berman and his entire staff at the National Endowment for the Humanities have been supportive in every aspect of this undertaking. The sponsors of the lecture in Washington, Chicago, and San Francisco made arrangements that were satisfactory in every way. My secretary, Margaret Fitzsimmons, and my research assistant, Joseph Castrovinci, were helpful in ways that went far beyond their assigned duties. My student Paul Finkelman generously offered many helpful suggestions. My wife gave the manuscript a critical reading and, as is her wont, tolerated me. To all of these I am deeply grateful.

Chicago, 17 May 1976   JOHN HOPE FRANKLIN

one

The Dream Deferred

On 28 August 1963, some 200,000 American citizens, black and white, converged on the nation's capital in the largest demonstration in the history of the United States. They gathered in the shadow of the Lincoln Memorial to present a "living petition" for jobs and freedom and equality. Among the several persons who presented the cause that they espoused, it was Martin Luther King who spoke most eloquently to the point of the traditional American dream of equality. He had a dream, he said, that one day the "sons of former slaves and the sons of former slaveholders will be able to sit down together at the table of brotherhood" and that "little black boys and black girls will be able to join hands with little white boys and white girls as sisters and brothers." This was merely the most recent expression of a sentiment that had been uttered, in one form or another, for more than three centuries.

Each generation of Americans, from the very first handful in the seventeenth century to the hundreds of millions in the twentieth century, has sought to create a social order in which equity and justice, as they understood it, would prevail. The Pilgrims in Massachusetts and the settlers in Virginia were matched in the vigor of their efforts by the ceaseless struggles of the Jeffersonians and Jacksonians and of the sectionalists and unionists of the nineteenth century. And this has surely been true of the numerous varieties of idealists and realists of our own time. Each individual and each group brought to this quest the varied backgrounds and experiences that defined their own objectives and fostered differences in methods as well as goals. On that August afternoon in 1963 Dr. King was defining the objectives of the group for which he spoke, and it goes without saying that there were others whose backgrounds and experiences prompted them to differ strongly with him in goals as well as methods.

Tensions and conflicts arising from these differences were inevitable, but in most cases— through the years—the participants demonstrated a remarkable capacity to resolve such difficulties. Religious conflicts gave way to a measure of toleration. Economic questions were mitigated by the numerous opportunities afforded by an expanding frontier as well as the diversity of economic pursuits. Political controversies moderated in the face of common enemies, the opportunity to explore alternatives on the local level, and common aspirations of self-determination. Perhaps neither perfect peace nor a perfect society would be achieved quickly, if ever; but the Americans moved toward a tolerable existence rather quickly, and this condition encouraged them to hope for and work for the higher goals.

One area which escaped the creative genius that had done so much to ease tensions in a dozen areas and chart the course for their ultimate solution was race. The problem was not with those troublesome native Americans, so strange and so different, who gave the colonists some moments of anxiety in the early years. Their strengths and weaknesses were soon accurately measured, and the formulas for their complete control or annihilation were worked out almost as soon. Nor was it with the several different groups of Europeans, whom Crèvecoeur, even in the Revolutionary years, would regard as belonging to different races. They were to be contrasted from the earlier settlers by their speech, their dress, their religion, or some other cultural attributes. But they had been known to each other and to the original colonists for centuries, and their membership in a common racial group was acknowledged by all but the most suspicious or the most uninformed. They could, moreover, accommodate themselves to each other by acts of mutual friendship and respect, including intermarriage.

But almost from the beginning such bonds of mutual friendship and respect were lacking in the relationship of Europeans and Africans in the New World. The decision to enslave Africans may well have been facilitated by an unfavorable assessment that Englishmen had already made before they settled in the New World. Surely the very act of enslavement served to generate still lower estimates of those held in bondage; and thus the twin acts of general debasement, as Winthrop Jordan in his *White over Black* calls slavery and prejudice, generated for blacks a status of degradation that remained operative for centuries. From the second decade of the seventeenth century to the eighth decade of the twentieth century this debasement would characterize race relations in this country. It could be seen in Virginia in 1642 when a magistrate sentenced a white indentured servant to an additional year of service for running away and a black indentured servant to labor for the remainder of his life for precisely the same offense. (In an interesting way certain absconding Negroes fared better by 1661, when a Virginia statute declared that when an "English servant shall run away in company with any negroes who are incapable of makeing satisfaction by addition of time" he was required to serve for the Negroes' lost time as well as his own.) And the distinction could also be seen in 1963 when the governor of Alabama stood in the door of the state university in an attempt to block the enrollment of a Negro student. Even more revealing—and disturbing—was that this single act of "statesmanship" earned for the governor the most serious consideration by millions of Americans as a candidate in three presidential campaigns!

It was not merely the commitment to the perpetual enslavement of Africans that set the English colonists apart from their brethren at home, where

6

the abhorrence of slavery was unequivocally expressed in 1773 by Lord Mansfield in the celebrated Somerset case. It was also the commitment to the principle of the inequality of blacks with whites, a condition that could not be significantly relieved even by emancipation, that seemed to confer on the colonists a special responsibility to promulgate and perpetuate the doctrine and practice of racial inequality. Free Negroes, whether or not they had ever been slaves, bore the burdens of inequality in a manner similar to that of slaves; and their inequality was likely to be clearly defined by law and custom that became all but universal. Differences in the punishment of whites and free blacks for the same offense, the prohibition against a free Negro's lifting his hand against a white person even in self defense, his exclusion from the militia, and his inclusion in the application of many parts of the slave code suggest that in the colonial years a black man who was *not* human chattel was nevertheless a human pariah.

The position of the colonists on African slavery was rendered extraordinarily difficult by the fact that human bondage was, as David B. Davis has observed, "an intrinsic part of American development from the first discoveries." Blacks had cleared the forests, felled the trees, drained the swamps, removed the boulders, and planted and harvested the crops. "To live in Virginia without slaves is morally impossible," an Anglican priest serving in the tidewater wrote his brother in London in 1757. Patrick Henry, who preferred death for himself if he could not have liberty, spoke almost casually of the "general inconvenience" of living in Virginia without slaves. By the end of the eighteenth century Negro slavery pervaded the atmosphere; and in many places where it did not flourish, as in Providence and Boston, the shippers and merchants grew wealthy on the profits from the slave trade. The longer this condition prevailed, the more difficult it would be to face up to the problem of slavery in a free society or to accommodate the institution of slavery to the ideology of the Revolution.

The decade before the beginning of hostilities between Britain and her colonies was one in which the colonists made the most eloquent statements of their rights. It was essential to their own freedom, they said, that "no taxes be imposed on them but with their own consent, given personally or by their representatives." The king's liege subjects in the colonies were entitled to "all the inherent rights and liberties of his natural born subjects within the kingdom of Great Britain," they cried. What is a man's own "is absolutely his own; and . . . no man hath a right to take it from him without his consent." The New York Sons of Liberty were subscribers "being influenced from a regard to liberty, and disposed to use all lawful endeavors in our power to defeat the pernicious project, and to transmit to our posterity, those blessings of freedom which our ancestors have handed down to us." If it was possible for men to believe that the "divine Author of our existence intended a part of the human race to hold an absolute property in, and an unbounded power over others ... the inhabitants of these colonies might at least require from the Parliament ... some evidence that this dreadful authority over them, has been granted to that body."

The situation was complicated by the fact that the colonists viewed themselves as slaves if they submitted to the policies England was imposing on them after 1763. Slavery was, in the words of Bernard Bailyn, "a crucial concept in eighteenth century political discourse. The ultimate political threat, the absolute political evil, it was embedded in the structure of political thought; it appears in every statement of political principle, in every discussion of constitutionalism or legal rights, in every exhortation to resistance." "Those who are taxed without their own consent are slaves," John Dickinson declared in his *Letters from a Farmer in Pennsylvania.* And yet, neither Dickinson nor any of his colleagues could accept such a lowly status or classify themselves in any sense with the Africans. The degraded status of the Africans was a dramatic and reprehensible reminder to the colonists of what the complete loss of freedom really meant. The mere thought was enough to embolden them not only to declare their independence but to fight for it.

When nothing could restrain the adversaries from armed conflict, there were several areas in which the colonists simply were not prepared for the consequences of the strong positions they had taken. They lacked an effective fighting force or even the military units that could be forged into one. They were without a real sense of mutual dependence or even a common purpose so necessary for nationhood. And the existence of slavery throughout the colonies, and especially among some of the most ardent patriots, compromised any arguments they dared to make regarding their own freedom from oppression. Circumstances required them to make the argument, but they could not possibly take it to the obvious conclusion, for that would be as damaging as it was logical.

There were some, nevertheless, who thought that it was not enough to fight in order to deliver themselves from the degradation of enslavement. For in the process they could not reconcile the institution of chattel slavery with a social order in which they were purchasing their own freedom, at least in part, with the labor of their bondsmen. "Does it follow," James Otis asked, "that 'tis right to enslave a man because he is black? Will short curled hair like wool instead of Christian hair ... help the argument? Can any logical inference in favor of slavery be drawn from a flat nose, a long or short face?" Richard Wells of Philadelphia wondered in 1774 how the colonists could "reconcile the exercise of SLAVERY with our *professions of freedom.*" In the same year Abigail Adams wrote her husband, "It always appeared a most iniquitous scheme to me to fight ourselves for what we are daily robbing and plundering from those who have as good a right to freedom as we have."

It appeared for a time that the arguments of the opponents of slavery were not only unassailable but might indeed become overpowering. Slaves themselves began pressing their masters to grant them the freedom that the patriots were seeking from Britain. A group of Massachusetts blacks "detained in a State of slavery in the Bowels of a free and Christian country," in pleading for their freedom in 1774 told the legislature that "Every Principle from which America has Acted in the Cours of their unhappy dificultes with Great Briton Pleads Stronger than A Thousand arguments in favours of your petioners." Samuel Hopkins echoed their pleas with great eloquence when he said that the slavery of which the colonists complained "is lighter than a feather compared to their [the Africans'] heavy doom, and may be called liberty and happiness when contrasted with the most abject slavery and inutterable wretchedness to which they are subjected."

Surely some white colonists as well as some slaves and free Negroes believed that the dream of universal freedom and equality, described so movingly by Otis, Hopkins, and others, would become a reality in the crucible of the revolutionary struggle. But the caveats offered by the faint-hearted as well as the resistance put up by those unalterably opposed to any change in the status of blacks was a clear indication that any change would be postponed indefinitely, if not forever. Patrick Henry confessed an "abhorrence of slavery" and found it difficult to understand how it could flourish "in a country, above all others, fond of liberty." But this was an

11

opinion expressed privately to a Quaker friend; and the public was protected from his righteous wrath. Samuel Adams was careful to heap strictures on Great Britain for every transgression of which the Mother Country was conceivably guilty; but he was just as careful not to speak out against slavery, presumably for the reason that it might "jeopardize the unity of the colonies." The colonists needed all the unity they could get, for clearly they were fighting for a set of principles that did not transcend race, principles which only Englishmen or Europeans, committed by habit and choice, could understand and appreciate.

If the principles for which the colonists fought did not transcend race, the question of race, nevertheless, would not die, even as the colonists declared their independence. And if anyone, among all the colonists, could cope with the question it was Thomas Jefferson. As a large slaveholder, Jefferson knew well the interests of those who held men in bondage. As a man of the Enlightenment, he had a deep appreciation of the meaning of freedom as a state of existence that could scarcely be determined on the basis of class or race. As a very sensitive human being, he knew the warmth and depth of a personal relationship that could indeed transcend race, as his personal servant, Isaac, has told us. That he had serious reservations about slavery was attested by his early, futile efforts, in 1769, to change the Virginia law of manumission to facilitate the master's emancipation of a slave. How deeply he regretted his failure we do not know.

As the author of the Declaration of Independence Jefferson once more sought to strike at the institution of slavery. In the first draft of the historic document the young Virginian penned what John Adams called "a vehement philippic" against Negro slavery. Blaming the king for crimes in this as in numerous other areas, Jefferson said, "He has waged cruel war against human nature itself, violating its most sacred rights of life and liberty in the persons of a distant people who never offended him, captivating and carrying them into slavery in another hemisphere, or to incur miserable death in their transportation thither."

This was an auspicious beginning in the attempt to bring the antislavery cause into the movement for independence. And in placing on the king the onus of slavery and the slave trade, Jefferson obviously hoped to win wide support since he had implicated neither the southern slaveholders nor the northern slave traders. But he succeeded only in convincing both groups that an institution so close to the heart of American social and economic life should not be thrown away by placing it on the royal doorstep where it might die or disappear, especially if the patriots won their independence. Consequently, the Continental Congress voted to expunge the "vehement philippic" from the Declaration. The record does not indicate that Jefferson made any effort to save the section over which he had labored so diligently.

In his lively little book, *The Declaration of Independence*, Carl Becker expressed pleasure that Congress omitted the passage on slavery and the slave trade altogether. He argues that the discrepancy between fact and representation was too flagrant, for George III was not responsible for maintaining slavery and the slave trade in the colonies. But the other charges against the king could hardly receive high grades for their fidelity to the facts either. Becker further argues that it is in this part of the Declaration that Jefferson "conspicuously failed to achieve literary excellence," because he was attempting to achieve something he was temperamentally unfitted to achieve. It lacks warmth, Becker contends; and there was in it "a sense of labored effort, of deliberate striving for an effect that does not come." The passage seems to me to be at least as eloquent and as passionate as those sections that refer to the quartering of soldiers in the homes of the colonists or the cutting off of colonial trade with other parts of the world. But whether or not it lacked literary felicity, it clearly lacked appeal to the slaveholders and slave traders and, thus, was totally unacceptable to them.

As the most important document of the Revolution and easily one of the most important statements on the rights of man ever published, it seems unfortunate that the Declaration of Independence, in its final form, said nothing at all about the widespread practice of trading in human flesh and holding human beings in perpetual bondage. And it is insufficient to dismiss the omission as a happy resolution of a dilemma occasioned by stylistic infelicities or even by the resistance of slave traders and slaveholders. The unwillingness of the Revolutionary leaders to regard human freedom as having some palpable connection with their own fight for political freedom stems from what Donald L. Robinson has referred to as the "marginal consideration given to Negro slavery by a people who thought of little else, publicly, but the political slavery that threatened to engulf them." That all men were created equal was a phrase so hypothetical, so philosophical, so abstract as to have little bearing on the day-to-day status of those who, by failing to resist, conspired in their own enslavement. For all its emphasis on natural equality and human liberty, the ideology of the American Revolution was not really egalitarian.

Perhaps Jefferson could not have done very much about it had he wanted to, and there is considerable doubt that he really wanted to. For although Jefferson insisted he was strongly anti-slavery, his antipathy toward the institution never took him to the point of freeing his own slaves or of using his enormous prestige to oppose slavery unequivocally in word or deed. His status as a large slaveholder and his constant preoccupation with financial matters led him, on occasion, to sell his slaves to pay off his debts and blurred the distinction between him and his fellow slaveholders who generally regarded capital in slaves as more important than Revolutionary ideology. Indeed, William Cohen has observed that Jefferson's wealth, "his status, and his political position were tied to the system of slavery" and to "a societal environment which took for granted the enslavement of one race by another."

Jefferson's most profound indictment of slavery was his assertion that he trembled for his country when, as he said, "I reflect that God is just; that his justice cannot sleep forever." And yet, if he cheered the process of gradual emancipation in the North, he did so in silence. If the abolition of slavery in the Northwest Territory in 1787 pleased him, there is no record of it, although he had advocated the same in 1784. Perhaps the most charitable thing that can be said is that he suffered the torment of an inner conflict created by his owning slaves on the one hand and having a moral repugnance to the institution of slavery on the other.

It was doubtless the view of Jefferson and many of his contemporaries that blacks were inferior to whites, and this had much to do with their inability or their unwillingness to take any significant steps against slavery. Even if blacks as well as whites were endowed by their creator with certain inalienable rights, it did not follow that a social revolution should be effected in order to secure those rights to blacks. For Jefferson was no more certain than many of his spiritual descendants some two hundred years later, in 1976, that the social order should accommodate itself to the complete or even substantial equality of blacks and whites.

In the eighteenth century this sense of racial inequality was as pervasive as slavery itself and was often used to justify keeping blacks in bondage. The student at the Harvard commencement in 1773 who argued that slavery did not violate the law of nature insisted Negroes were inferior to whites and for the good of all they should be kept in subordination. And since the typical African was, in his view, part idiot, part madman, and part child, his consent was not required before exercising authority over him. "Why," he asked, "should anyone interfere with a stable and beneficent social order, just to pursue some mystical primeval equality?"

Perhaps Jefferson would never have been so gauche or so candid as the brash young commencement debater; but his views on the inequality of the races were not very different. He set forth his views on the subject in his *Notes on Virginia*, written in 1781 for a limited private circulation and then reluctantly published by Jefferson when he realized that its contents were already becoming widely known. In defending a proposal in a draft of the revised Virginia code to deport slaves as they were emancipated, Jefferson saw no alternative. Should Negroes remain in the state, "deep-rooted prejudices" entertained by whites, "ten thousand recollections, by the blacks, of the injuries they have sustained; new provocations; the real distinctions which nature has made; and many other circumstances, will divide us into parties, and produce convulsions, which will probably never end but in the extermination of one or the other race." To these considerations he added others, including "physical and moral."

Jefferson found the skin color and other physical features of Africans unattractive and lacking in beauty. He asked, "Are not the fine mixtures of red and white, the expressions of every passion by greater or less suffusions of color in the one, preferable to that eternal monotony, which reigns in the countenance, that immovable veil of black which covers the emotions of the other race?" There followed a discussion in which Jefferson argued that the flowing hair and physical features of the whites were more attractive than those of blacks. He contended, moreover, that since blacks secrete less by the kidneys, and more by the glands of the skin, they have a "very strong and disagreeable odor." The nineteenth- and twentieth-century proponents of physiological differences between whites and blacks would not be able to put the case more succinctly or more crudely.

Jefferson thought he saw the mental and moral differences just as clearly and, if anything, attached more importance to them. Negroes, he said, required less sleep and thus, even after a hard day's work they could be induced by the slightest amusements to sit up until midnight. Yet, since their existence appeared to "participate more of sensation than reflection," they are disposed to sleep "when abstracted from their diversions, or unemployed in labor," like an animal whose body is at rest. "They are more ardent after their female," Jefferson was certain, "but love seems to them to be more an eager desire, than a tender delicate mixture of sentiment and sensation." In this connection one must recall that more than once Jefferson expressed a strong commitment only to those findings based on scientific observation. In memory, he said, "they are equal to whites; in reason much inferior, as I think one could scarcely be found capable of tracing and comprehending the investigations of Euclid."

Jefferson said he never found a black man who "had uttered a thought above the level of plain narration; never saw even an elementary trait of painting or sculpture." In purporting to use the language of natural history in discussing blacks, yet seeking to save himself from its rigorous axioms, Daniel J. Boorstin points out, Jefferson played "fast and loose with the concepts on which he had built his whole science." It would seem hardly likely that anyone with such pronounced views on the inferiority of blacks who, at the same time, believed blacks and whites could not live together as free persons could entertain a deeply serious belief that slaves should be emancipated.

For a new nation with extremely limited resources, the repatriation of three quarters of a million former slaves in their African homeland was beyond the wildest dreams of any eighteenth-century visionary. And since the deep-rooted prejudices of the whites and the "ten thousand recollections" by the blacks of the injuries they had sustained made it virtually impossible for manumitted slaves to remain within the country, exhortations against slavery were similar to a papal bull against the comet, to use Lincoln's apt phrase. If such views were held by Jefferson, whose natural sensibilities had been strengthened by the Enlightenment, it seems inconceivable that his less enlightened associates would have been more disposed to embrace antislavery views.

The view of the inferiority of blacks which was apparently held by most colonists did not relate merely to slaves but to all blacks, including those who were free. And the concept of racial inferiority was translated into law and custom which denied to free persons of color the minimum rights which other free persons enjoyed. Even before the Revolution any treatment of free blacks as equals was accidental or on a hit-or-miss basis. Limits were placed on Negro suffrage, and at best the colonial policy had a patchwork design, as Ira Berlin puts it in his *Slaves without Masters.* In the early eighteenth century, North and South Carolina barred free Negroes from the polls. By the time that Georgia joined in the proscription in 1761, North Carolina had reversed its position.

Blacks were officially excluded from the militia in all four New England colonies, but in practice they frequently served. Maryland excluded them, but Virginia allowed them to serve without arms. In some colonies they were barred from testifying against white persons, and in some they were taxed more heavily than whites or were prohibited from owning real estate. In dozens of other ways they suffered from legal distinctions and discriminations against them, not because they were not free but because they were not white.

Thus, at the time of the Revolution it was of doubtful significance to declare that blacks, free blacks, had been created equal when already the law that was written by the Patriots or their forebears had taken away those rights with which their Creator had endowed them. Free blacks, persuaded that their status conferred on them the right to bear arms against the enemy, were dismayed when the council of war, presided over by George Washington, in Cambridge in October 1775, excluded them from serving in the Continental Army. They had fought at Lexington and Concord and at Bunker Hill. Only their vigorous protest late in the year, together with the Patriots' fear that they would answer Lord Dunmore's call for them to join the British, brought forth a reversal of policy. There ensued, however, a long period in which states, acting on their own, excluded slaves or free blacks or both from service. Only the sagging fortunes of the Patriots' cause and the persistence of blacks in the assertion of their right to fight broke down the desire of the Americans to maintain an exclusively white man's army in the field.

Free Negroes also had to fight for their right, as taxpayers, to participate in the affairs of government. As property owners in Massachusetts, Paul and John Cuffe resented their exclusion from the suffrage and other citizenship rights. In a petition to the General Court in 1780 the Cuffe brothers, pointing out that they had "no vote or influence in the election with those that tax us," asked to be relieved from the duty of paying taxes. As a part of their running battle with the authorities, these two black brothers had refused to pay their taxes in 1778, 1779, and 1780. On his copy of the petition of 1780 John Cuffe wrote, "This is a copy of the petitions which we did deliver unto the honorable council and house for relief from taxation in the days of our distress. But we received none."

Accordingly, the authorities issued a warrant for the arrest of the Cuffe brothers. They were taken to the common jail in Taunton from which, after two hours, they were released on a writ of habeas corpus. After delays and postponements of their trial the young dissidents reluctantly agreed to pay their taxes and court costs in June 1781, and their case was dismissed. Four months before the British surrendered at Yorktown, Virginia, the free Negro brothers had surrendered at Taunton, Massachusetts. What they gave up had been a central issue in the war. The claim of no taxation without representation clearly did not extend to them.

It may be understandable, if regrettable, that the colonists could not bring themselves to incorporate the principles of human freedom into their struggle for political independence. After all, property was a central consideration in their immediate struggle;

and to have taken a stand against slavery would be to take a stand against the very principle for which they perceived themselves to be fighting. As David Brion Davis has observed, a free society was by no means incompatible with dependent classes of workers. He could have added, of course, that a truly free society *is* incompatible with a slave society, one consisting not merely of dependent workers, but of chattel slaves, unless some free men in that society are so callous as to define freedom in a way that denies it to one-fourth of the population. In any case, the colonists had come to terms with a definition of their social order in which freedom was to be ensured to those who already had it; and the risk of undermining the entire social order, and especially property rights, was too great to extend it to human beings who happened to be property.

This explains not only the attitude toward slavery of the colonists and the Revolutionary leaders but the attitude of the framers of the Constitution as well. By 1787 the institution of slavery was more deeply entrenched than ever in the five slave states of the South. Meanwhile, some steps had been taken to arrange for the gradual abolition of slavery in some of the Northern states.

But even in the North the rhetoric of freedom was related to the dependence of Massachusetts, Connecticut, and Rhode Island manufacturers of rum and the elaborately organized program and practice of the merchants and shippers on slavery and the slave trade. Small wonder that they tolerated, even supported, provisions in the new Constitution to return fugitive slaves to their owners and to permit the slave trade for at least another twenty years. Of the slave trade provision, James Wilson, the learned delegate from Pennsylvania who had wanted to end the slave trade completely, acquiesced. He said, "If there was no other lovely feature in the Constitution but this one, it would diffuse a beauty over its whole countenance." Then, he confidently but naively predicted that since new states would be under the control of Congress, slavery would never be introduced among them.

It was one thing to reconcile the rhetoric of political freedom to the maintenance of Negro slavery, as incongruous as it may appear to the liberal, enlightened, or merely logical mind. It was quite another to withhold the elementary rights of political and economic freedom from persons—in this case, black persons—who were already free or who were becoming free. And yet this is precisely what the new national government and most of the state governments were doing. In 1790 Congress enacted a law limiting naturalization to white aliens, thus suggesting that blacks who were imprudent enough to enter the United States could not expect ever to become citizens. In 1792 Congress authorized the organization of a militia and restricted enrollment to ablebodied white citizens, thus declaring to the 5,000 Negroes who had fought in the War for Independence that their services were no longer required. In 1802 Congress, in a law signed by Jefferson, excluded blacks from carrying the United States mail, a gratuitous expression of distrust of free Negroes or an indication that mail carriers occupied a position of social respectability that should not be violated by the presence of blacks. And to confuse the issue completely, the House of Representatives in 1803 passed a resolution to inquire into the expediency "of granting protection to such American seamen citizens of the United States, as are free persons of color."

When Congress undertook the task of establishing a government for the new capital at Washington, it made certain that free blacks were not only excluded from participating in the affairs of that government but also that they would be reminded constantly of their degraded position. It specified that only free white males were eligible to be the mayor or to sit on the Board of Aldermen or the Board of the Common Council. The franchise, moreover, was restricted to free white males. The Board of Aldermen and other officials were to "restrain and prohibit the nightly and other disorderly meetings of slaves, free negroes, and mulattoes, and to punish such slaves by whipping . . . or by imprisonment not exceeding three months . . . and to punish free negroes and mulattoes, by penalties not exceeding twenty dollars for any one offence, and in case of the inability of such free negro or mulatto to pay such penalty and cost thereon, to cause him or her to be confined to labor for anytime not exceeding six calendar months." No state or local government, from whatever part of the country at whatever time in the nineteenth or twentieth century could have been more unequivocal than the First, Second, Eleventh, and Sixteenth Congresses of the United States in making certain that free persons who were also black were deprived of every semblance of equality within the legal and political system.

This is the new federal government that had pushed through the very first Congress the bill of rights that so many critics had demanded as they considered the ratification of the new Constitution. This was the new federal government dominated by Washington, Jefferson, Adams, Hamilton, Madison, Gallatin, Monroe, and other fighters for the rights of men. This was the new federal government to which the state and local governments were beginning to look for guidance on such matters as equal rights and even-handed justice. The example was there as far as racial equality was concerned, and most of them followed it, especially since it was consonant with practices they were already following.

In Massachusetts, where the question of Negro suffrage was unclear and where, as we have seen, two free persons of color had been jailed because they protested against being deprived of the ballot in 1781, there was general hostility to black aliens. And following the guidelines laid down in federal legislation, Boston authorities in 1800 ordered the immediate deportation of 240 Negroes from the state. In New Jersey they could be banished from the state if convicted of any crime more serious than petty larceny, and in any case they could not travel beyond their home county without a certificate proving their freedom. Even in the new state of Ohio, a law of 1807 barred free Negroes unless they presented a court certificate as evidence of their freedom and posted a $500 bond guaranteeing their good behavior. Even where slavery was dead or dying, racial equality did not exist; and there was no indication that the country was the least bit interested in moving toward it.

People who experience unequal treatment because of their race, religion, or national origin and are generally powerless to secure protection of the law, frequently look to some informal arrangement, some gesture of sympathetic understanding, or some custom that may grant them relief. And there are times when, as a result of the compassion, outrage, or whim of the more powerful, they are successful. The pages of history are filled with such acts of simple justice, without which life would hardly be tolerable for the despised and disinherited. But by the very nature of things, such hapless supplicants are just as often rejected in their quest for some expression of understanding on the part of persons or groups more advantageously placed. This happened so often to free persons of color that at times many must have been driven to the point of desperation.

By the time the Constitution was written in Philadelphia, the free blacks of that city, numbering about

2,500, were a solid and stable element in the community. They performed all kinds of domestic and common labor and much of the skilled labor. There were, moreover, some notable leaders, such as James Derham, whom Benjamin Rush called a "very learned" physician, Richard Allen, a talented spiritual leader of his people, and James Forten, a well-to-do sail maker, whom Anthony Benezet described as "a gentleman by nature, easy in manner and able in intercourse." They compared favorably with any other small, distinctive group in a city of almost a hundred thousand; and it was reasonable for them to expect civil treatment.

Richard Allen is credited with having increased Negro attendance at St. George's Methodist Episcopal Church in Philadelphia. When he began to use the facilities of the church for morning services at five o'clock, before the blacks reported for duty in the white homes, there was no objection. Indeed, his religious zeal was praised by the elders and trustees. As the number of Negroes attending regular services increased, however, the white members took steps to separate the blacks from the whites. First, blacks were seated in the rear and on the sides, but apparently this separation was not sufficient from the point of view of the whites.

In November 1787 it was announced that Negroes who attended St. George's would be seated in the gallery. When Allen and his group arrived they dutifully went to the gallery and proceeded to sit on the front rows. As they knelt to join in the prayer that was in progress, the white trustees began to tug at them, commanding them to move to the rear seats in the gallery. The blacks requested permission to complete their prayers, but the whites would not relent. When the prayers were over, as Allen reported, "all [of the blacks] went out of the church in a body and they were no more plagued with us in the church." Two months after the Constitution had been completed in Philadelphia, there was little evidence of Christian brotherhood in the City of Brotherly Love.

One can speculate on whether the denial of equality to a group is more painful to its members than it is to an individual who is singled out for such dubious distinction. If the group experiences the pain of humiliation, it can unite and take steps to protect its members from a repetition of the experience. That is what Allen and his group did in founding Bethel African Methodist Episcopal Church. Benjamin Banneker had no such recourse, and his bitterness over slights and condescension is abundantly clear in his writings. Banneker, a Maryland free Negro, had become quite proficient in mathematics and astronomy and in March 1791 had been engaged to assist in surveying the new District of Columbia. Although Jefferson, as Secretary of State, had some role in selecting persons to survey the District, Banneker could hardly have been unacquainted with the Secretary's views on the inferiority of Negroes. Perhaps he had not read the *Notes on Virginia*, already in print for almost a decade. But he would surely have been aware that the announcement of his own appointment in the Georgetown *Weekly Ledger* hailed it as proof that "Mr. Jefferson's concluding that that race of men were void of mental endowment was without foundation."

When Banneker published his first almanac in the fall of 1791, he sent Jefferson a copy. In an accompanying, polite letter he could not conceal his bitterness, some of which must have been occasioned by his knowledge of Jefferson's racial views. He appealed to Jefferson to "embrace every opportunity, to eradicate that train of absurd and false ideas and opinions that blacks were scarcely capable of mental endowments which so generally prevails with respect to us." To make certain Jefferson felt the full burden of his responsibilities as a white man and as a slaveholder, Banneker reminded him it was "the indispensable duty of those, who maintain for themselves the right of human nature, and who possess the obligations of Christianity, to extend their power and influence to the relief of every part of the human race, from whatever burden or oppression they may unjustly labor under." Banneker did not presume to tell Jefferson by what methods the black people could be relieved of their degradation but he did recommend that "you and all others . . . wean yourselves from those narrow prejudices which you have imbibed."

Jefferson sent a courteous but ambiguous letter of thanks in which he assured Banneker that "No body wishes more than I do to see such proofs as you exhibit, that nature has given to our black brethren, talents equal to those of the other colors of men." In sending the almanac to his friend the Marquis de Condorcet, he noted that he would be delighted to see "these instances of moral eminence so multiplied as to prove to them that the want of talents observed in them is merely the effect of their degraded condition, and not proceeding from any difference in the structure of the parts on which intellect depends." Since Jefferson, of all people, held firmly to the view that the "moral sense" and the faculties of intellect were two quite separate entities, I am inclined to agree with Winthrop Jordan that what Jefferson said "simply made no sense."

Jefferson had his doubts not only about the mental capabilities of blacks but also about their intellectual honesty. He had told Condorcet about "very elegant solutions of Geometrical problems" by Banneker, but he told his friend Joel Barlow that Banneker's work was "not without suspicion of aid from Ellicot," Banneker's white friend and sponsor. He had cast a similar doubt regarding Phillis Wheatley, the Negro poetess, by discussing her poems as works "written under her name." In any case he declared that she was not a poet, but twenty years later he admitted that "of all men I am the last who should undertake to decide as to the merits of poetry." One would have thought that Jefferson could not have it both ways, but apparently he thought that he could.

There were later occasions when Jefferson's position on the problem of race made no sense. During his presidency he maintained a discreet silence on all matters pertaining to slavery, insisting that "Should an occasion ever occur in which I can interpose with decisive effect, I shall certainly know and do my duty with promptitude and zeal." The time never came. After he left the presidency, he declined to speak out, insisting that his views "had long since been in possession of the public," and in any case the younger generation seemed apathetic on the subject. Earlier, however, when he asserted that the cause of emancipation had the support of "nearly the whole of the young men as fast as they come into public life" he never even acknowledged the existence of the Virginia Abolition Society.

When Jefferson retired to Monticello and his exquisite surroundings and his vast retinue of slaves, he argued that the enterprise of opposing slavery was for the young. In 1785 he had expressed the hope that the way was preparing "under the auspices of heaven, for a total emancipation." By 1820 he could only despair that in the controversy over Missouri, Americans had a "wolf by the ears, and we can neither hold him, nor safely let him go. Justice is in one scale, and self-preservation in the other." It is clear that for Jefferson self-preservation was uppermost in his mind.

In some far-off day, perhaps, Americans would be courageous enough and strong enough to take the wolf by the ears and subdue him. Meanwhile, there was very little that could be done except to follow the counsel that Jefferson gave to Edward Coles, one of his young protégés, to remain in Virginia and take good care of his slaves. "I hope . . . you will reconcile yourself to your country and its unfortunate condition." If this was the best that the Revolution's quintessential egalitarian had to offer, one could hardly expect any better dream of equality from his fellows. New York's James Tallmadge had a better dream in 1819, when he sought to exclude slavery from the new state of Missouri. With the defect of slavery and inequality, Tallmadge told his colleagues in the House of Representatives, "your Government must crumble to pieces, and your people become the scoff of the world." Jefferson called the proposal a cheap Federalist party trick. "The leaders of federalism," he asserted, "defeated in their schemes of obtaining power by rallying partisans to the principle of monarchism . . . have changed their tack, and thrown out another barrel to the whale." One difficulty with Jefferson's analysis was that Tallmadge, who wanted to prohibit the spread of slavery, was not a Federalist but a member of Jefferson's own party! Whatever the motives of the Northerners—Democrats or Federalists—it was hardly becoming to one who for almost fifty years had been waiting for the opportunity to strike a blow for freedom to say, once again, that the time was not yet ripe.

The issue was as confusing fifty years after the Declaration of Independence as it had been in 1776. When men argued that blacks were innately inferior, they were not addressing the point at issue. It was, of course, unseemly for men of the Enlightenment, ardent in their adherence to the principles of science, to discuss texture of hair and alleged body odors as sound bases on which to make decisions regarding the fate of a people. When there were scarcely any opportunities for Negroes to learn to read and write and cipher, it would not seem to be a profound discovery that they could not trace and comprehend the investigations of Euclid. But the real point at issue was twofold: The first was whether slaves should be treated as property or men. If they were men, Gouverneur Morris had said to the Constitutional Convention, then make them citizens and let them vote. The view of Virginia's George Mason and his supporters prevailed, however, and the Constitution did nothing to indicate that blacks were equal to others in the enjoyment of their rights.

The second point was whether blacks who were free should be treated as other free persons. In the first fifty years of the nation's history the dominant view was that they should not be. In the South free Negroes were nothing less than pariahs, while in the North they were an oppressed and underprivileged minority. Even if men did not violate the Constitution in maintaining slavery, they clearly violated it in denying full citizenship rights to free blacks.

The Revolutionary dream of equality of all peoples was deferred by the necessity, as the Founding Fathers saw it, of protecting the inviolability of property and maintaining a stable social order. It was also deferred because of the pervasive view that a man not only had to be free, but also white, in order to enjoy equality or even to aspire to it. Perhaps the men of the Revolution, in passing on to some later generation the task of solving the problem of race, did not know how difficult it would become in later years. It remained for those living two centuries later to discover that the intervening years would render the problem even more difficult to solve.

In this Bicentennial year, sixty-two windows were broken in the Chicago home of a young black nurse, who discovered that her property was not inviolable when it happened to be in a neighborhood whose ethnic purity was threatened by her presence. That same week our government warned Cuba against engaging in adventures in Africa, but no one warned the domestic hoodlums or even reminded them that the Revolution was fought to protect private property if not human freedom. In this Bicentennial year a black citizen of Boston was beaten up by white hoodlums near the city hall. When the mayor observed the bleeding man, whom he knew, he warned him that when it was *his* turn to be on top, he should deal more kindly with the Puerto Ricans than he had been dealt with. The mayor, who recounted the incident on public television, did not indicate whether or not his black friend responded. But the victim could have told the mayor that for two hundred years his black ancestors had been waiting their turn not to be on top or to engage in violence but merely to experience the inalienable right of equality. Each succeeding wave of newcomers had in time moved ahead of the blacks to the point where they could enjoy that dignity of existence that only equality in a free society can provide. For him and his ancestors the dream of equality was always deferred.

What happens to a dream deferred?

> Does it dry up
> like a raisin in the sun?
> Or fester like a sore—
> And then run?
> Does it stink like rotten meat?
> Or crust and sugar over—
> like a syrupy sweet?
>
> Maybe it just sags
> like a heavy load.
>
> Or does it explode?

Focused on History
lot on Thomas Jeff.

two

The Old Order Changeth Not

The remarkable thing about the problem of racial equality is the way it has endured and remained topical. It was discussed in the taverns and meeting places of eighteenth-century Williamsburg. It became an obsessive preoccupation of Americans in the nineteenth century. It was discussed at the 1976 meeting of the American Association for the Advancement of Science. Indeed, virtually anything pertaining to race qualifies as a problem, and at times it can be curiously amusing. Thirty years ago I was having luncheon in Philadelphia with a white Princeton professor and his wife. They were intimate friends of mine and the occasion was a sort of reunion. Toward the end of the meal the waiter delivered to the Princeton professor a note from two white ladies sitting in another part of the restaurant. The note, which he showed to me after we finished our meal, simply said, "We, too, are interested in the race problem. We wish you much success." It was left unclear just what my friends had undertaken that elicited the support of the two ladies.

Whenever and wherever the matter arose—in

whatever century, in whatever place—the nature and urgency of the problem, the underlying assumptions, and the difficulties in the way of resolving it satisfactorily were amazingly similar. When the Revolutionary leaders removed racial equality from their agenda and declared that, perhaps, some later generation would be better able to deal with it, they were passing on essentially what their forebears had bequeathed to them. When the entire matter was again explored in 1820, during the debates over whether Missouri should be admitted as a slave or a free state, the bitterness engendered between the North and the South indicated that the solution was no closer than it had been a century earlier.

But for most Americans—and certainly for those whose views prevailed—it was a quite simple problem. Slavery was, they conceded, a "fixed evil" which they could not eliminate, but emancipation would only alleviate the problem of race while at the same time underscoring the impossibility of equality. For, once emancipated, Dr. Thomas Cooper insisted, free Negroes would become "the most idle, debauched, thievish and insolent" group of people that one had ever seen in the United States. Robert Reid of Georgia said he would hail the day "as the most glorious in its dawning, which should behold, with safety to themselves and our citizens, the black population of the United States placed upon the high eminence of equal rights." But this, he hastened to add, was a "wild dream of philanthropy which can never be fulfilled; and whoever shall act in this country upon such wild theories shall cease to be a benefactor, and become a destroyer of the human family." Whether the wild dream could ever be fulfilled remained to be seen; but the admission of Missouri as a slave state and the bitterness that surfaced during the controversy was not a good portent for the resolution of the problem of race in the foreseeable future.

Proslavery advocates could exult over the victory of Missouri's becoming a slave state. This was the sixth slave state to enter the Union since the ratification of the Constitution. Thus, the expectation of some framers of the document that no slave states would ever be admitted must be regarded as naive indeed. Those in the South who were committed to racial inequality rejoiced over the embarrassment the Northerners experienced when, in the course of the Missouri debates, it was revealed how blacks were oppressed in the North. This did not mean, however, that the victory of the advocates of racial inequality was complete and permanent. In the wake of the settlement of the Missouri question several developments seemed to augur well for those who did not wish to postpone indefinitely the dream of full equality regardless of racial or other considerations. At least these developments could create conditions which would subject the problem of equality to the severest test the people of the United States had yet experienced. Perhaps some positive and significant steps toward equality could well be taken.

The years from 1820 to 1840 were a period in which it seemed that the idea of equality could flourish and bear fruit. Workers in the emerging industrial order were demanding a more equitable share of the returns from their labor. "What but a principle of slavery," one of them asked, "could have made it a felony for a working man to demand the true and just wages for his labour?" Even if they did not have black workers in mind, the principle could hardly be confined to white workers, for the spirit of equality was in the air. The Jacksonians themselves conveyed the impression that the common man was as entitled to equality as any person of privilege. "In a free government," the *Mechanics Free Press* said in 1829, "no artificial distinctions or inequalities ought to be tolerated by law, inasmuch as the first principle of nature as well as republicanism is, that all men are born equally free and independent." Could it be that the stirring words of the Declaration of Independence would finally be transformed into reality?

The impulse for reform in the 1820s and 1830s was all but universal. Immigrants coming to the New World in increasing numbers sought in their adopted home the equality that had eluded them in Europe. The assurances they received that freedom, equality, and justice would be theirs forever were as heartwarming as they were refreshing. There was, moreover, a veritable groundswell of sympathy and support for the blind, the insane, the poor, the orphans, and others who were disadvantaged. Mere benevolence was not enough, one humanitarian declared, for the aim of the higher benevolence was "to unite men as a family of brothers."

Meanwhile, there were stirrings among women,

who began to speak out against the thousand invidious distinctions to which they were subjected by law and custom. Abigail Adams, Hanna Lee Corbin, Mercy Otis Warren, and other women of the Revolutionary era had been firm but unsuccessful in their stand for equal rights for women. The legacy of no compromise they passed on was taken up and vigorously promoted by Margaret Fuller, Susan B. Anthony, Lucy Stone, and many others. In seeking to break down the barriers against them, they joined in the struggle against human bondage, against economic discrimination of every kind, and against those institutions and practices, such as the saloon, male suffrage, and property laws which added to the stresses between the sexes and among the various classes of society.

There were indications, moreover, that the goal of political equality, at least for white males, was within reach. Early in the nineteenth century the freehold requirement was removed in most states, while the less difficult taxpaying qualification was disappearing in some communities. By 1825 virtually all major restrictions on the vote of white adult males had been removed in all states except Rhode Island, Louisiana, Mississippi, and Virginia. The secret ballot was gaining in favor, and it replaced voice voting in some places. While it is not accurate to state, as Tocqueville did, that in America men without property ruled, it is fair to say that a climate favoring political equality among white men was improving markedly.

Current religious and philosophical thought was

likewise impatient with presumed distinctions among men. To those who had hoped the New World society would reject the values that emphasized material things at the expense of humane aspirations, the choice was clear. They would lay their emphasis on the exaltation of man, all men, and would place little stock in the Yankee trait of materialism. The important thing, those Transcendentalists thought, was the daily rebirth of God in each individual soul. Each man and woman, by virtue of being identical with nature, was entitled to enjoy equal rights and privileges. The mind and spirit must be rescued from human exploitation and inequality. Thus, from the point of view of Theodore Parker and other leading Transcendentalists, slavery as well as other distinctions based on race or religion could have no place in a society where each individual should cherish the divine spark within himself.

The institution of slavery itself, moreover, was coming under the most sustained assault yet made on it in the United States. In increasing numbers individuals were speaking out against slavery. Free Negroes such as Robert A. Young and David Walker attacked the institution in a fashion that must have shocked even those who supported them. Walker, the North Carolina free black who had moved to Boston, insisted that every black man had a right to his freedom and all other rights that other Americans enjoyed. He even cited the Declaration of Independence to support his argument that blacks were justified in resisting, by force if necessary, the oppression of whites. Young and Walker were joined by such white worthies as William Lloyd Garrison, who dedicated his life to the abolition of slavery, and Lydia Maria Child, who, in 1834, said that "even if it could be proved that negro blood inevitably produces stupidity in the brain, who would be absurd enough to say that the civil and social rights of mankind must be regulated according to the measure of genius?" Every white person below the level of genius had something to ponder!

Soon, antislavery organizations were attracting attention as they railed against human bondage and equated slaveholders with the lowest form of human existence. Garrison shouted from the housetops as well as from the pages of *The Liberator*, saying he would be as harsh as truth and as uncompromising as justice in his holy crusade against slavery. Frederick Douglass, the runaway slave, became one of the most eloquent opponents of slavery. After speaking against slavery all across the North, Douglass went to England in order, he said, "to tear off the mask from this abominable system, to expose it to the light of heaven, aye, to the heat of the sun, that it may burn and wither it out of existence." In American cities and hamlets the white and black evangelists of abolition preached their gospel, calling on all Americans to renounce the "vile evil" of slavery. By 1840 the abolitionists were not only appealing to the consciences of Americans but to those who aspired to hold public office; and they began a widespread effort to elect only those who were committed to the abolition of slavery.

What a contrast this seemed to be to the old order which during the Revolution embraced human slavery even as the Patriots fought for political freedom. How different the mood seemed to be from that of the framers of the Constitution, who guaranteed the perpetuation of slavery even as they sought to form a more perfect union. It was even different from the mood of those who admitted Missouri as a slave state and permitted the spread of slavery into the southern part of the Louisiana Purchase. It was the new spirit of "no compromise" that seemed to indicate a turning away from the old order and a determination to build a society of equals.

These, however, were largely appearances, and they did not seem to recognize fully the powerful forces in the land—some new, some old—that would resist to the death any significant changes in the old order as far as blacks were concerned. Among them were the advocates of states' rights who would transform the notion of confederation into a mighty bulwark against federal intervention in the master-slave relationship. There were, moreover, the supporters of slavery who would take the relatively innocuous eighteenth-century affirmations of the institution and build them into an incredibly powerful defense of human bondage. There were also the new pseudo-scientists who would take Jefferson's awkward assertions about the inferiority of blacks and raise them to the level of indisputable scientific "truths." It would be difficult indeed to change the old order in the face of such formidable obstacles.

The new Constitution of 1787 greatly strengthened the central government, but the legacy of confederation continued to encourage those who feared the consequences of unbridled power in Washington. Perhaps it was all right for Congress to end the slave trade in 1808, but the fight over Missouri clearly demonstrated to Southerners what lay in store for them if they were not ever vigilant to the encroachment of federal power. Many persons, jealous of the power that the states enjoyed, thought it improper for Congress to discuss slavery or even to receive petitions against it. In 1838 John Calhoun insisted the states had "the exclusive and sole right over their own domestic institutions and police" and that any intermeddling with them by any one or more states was an "assumption of superiority not warranted by the Constitution, insulting to the States interfered with, tending to endanger their domestic peace and tranquility, subversive of the object for which the Constitution was formed, and by necessary consequence, tending to weaken and destroy the Union itself." Such views left little room in which those who differed could search for a position of conciliation.

Every state had a right to protect itself against subversion, even if that subversion was perpetrated by the central government, Southerners began to say. Attacks on slavery were clearly subversive, as

Calhoun and dozens of his Southern colleagues argued; and it was the right of every state to take whatever action it deemed necessary to arrest such subversive activities. It could take the form of enacting laws against the circulation of antislavery materials or of burning them when transmitted through the mails. It could mean preventing the reading of antislavery petitions in Congress or threatening to dissolve the Union if Northern radicals persisted in attempting to push through Congress laws and resolutions looking toward Negro equality. The rights of the states to protect slavery, if Congress would not do so, and to enact laws recognizing the differences between blacks and whites must be protected at all costs, even if it meant dissolving the Union.

The Founding Fathers, claiming that a bitter confrontation with the supporters of slavery would endanger the very life of the new nation, had passed on to the next generation—or the next—the unenviable task of extending human equality to non-whites. When they did so, with an air of optimism and relief in their voices and in their words, they seem not to have even a casual appreciation of the remarkably strong hold slavery already had on hundreds of thousands of Americans or of the profound importance of slavery to the nation's economy, North as well as South. They soon found out. When the abolitionists began their crusade, the alacrity with which so many sprang to the defense of slavery should have been proof enough that the task of abolishing slavery and wiping out racial inequality had become infinitely more difficult than it had appeared in earlier years. Before the abolitionists knew what had happened or before the bystanders could follow the game plan as it unfolded, a whole set of complex and presumably unassailable arguments in favor of slavery and racial inequality had been advanced.

Slavery was justified on the basis of historical precedent. "The free states of antiquity abounded with slaves," declared George Fitzhugh, the leading theoretician of the Southern social order. And what was good for the Greeks and Romans was good for the Virginians and South Carolinians. The institution of slavery had "received the sanction of the Almighty in the Patriarchal age," the Reverend Thornton Stringfellow asserted, "and its legality was recognized by Jesus Christ in his Kingdom." Cotton is king, proclaimed David Christy; and since his majesty is acquainted with the secret springs of human action, "he has no evidence that colored men can grow his cotton but in the capacity of slaves"; consequently, it will be his policy to defeat all schemes of emancipation. In all social systems there must be a class to perform the menial tasks, said James Henry Hammond; and Africans were perfectly suited to perform those tasks.

And so the defense went on. But the most remarkable of all these remarkable defenses argued that blacks were inferior in virtually all the traits which were the prerequisites for freedom and equality. Consequently, slavery was a happy solution, the only solution, if such inferior people were to be permitted to remain among free, superior people. Negroes, said Dr. Samuel Cartwright, the distinguished New Orleans physician, had more acute senses than the whites, approximating in this regard the lower animals. They could, for example, detect snakes by the sense of smell; while their strong odor, which had been so obnoxious to Thomas Jefferson, was an indication of "high health, happiness, and good treatment." Their brain development, claimed Louis Agassiz, one of the nation's leading scientists, "never got beyond that observable in a Caucasian in boyhood" and bore a striking resemblance "in several particulars to the brain of an ourang-outang."

The orangutan had been the favorite object with which to compare Negroes from the time Jefferson said that black men preferred white women just as the orangutan preferred black women to females of his own species. This was as unlikely in terms of the findings of Agassiz as it was crude in terms of the observations of Jefferson. It is not clear that Agassiz based his "findings" on any scientific examination. He had no blacks in his household. Jefferson, on the other hand, had been around blacks all his life; but it is unlikely he would have explained to visitors the presence of mulattoes in his own household with a sigh of resignation that "black gentlemen preferred blondes."

Nor could Dr. Cartwright explain the intellectual attainments of the physician James Derham, the astronomer Benjamin Banneker, the academician John

Chavis, or the abolitionist orator and editor Frederick Douglass by asserting that their brains could be compared with that of an orangutan. This was a rhetorical flourish that reflected the barrenness as well as the desperation of those who advanced the proslavery argument. They would even insist that there were certain qualities of temperament and physique that disposed blacks to be happier in the warm, Southern climate and more efficient when under the benign but solicitous supervision of a white master. There were even certain diseases peculiar to the Negro, such as drapetomania which impelled him to run away at certain times of the year. No straw, however fast it flew in the wind, was too elusive to be grasped by these desperate degraders of human beings. Thus, theology, science, economics, and philosophy were at the command of those who mounted a comprehensive program to thwart any move or impulse toward racial equality.

In arguing that Negroes were inferior to whites, Southern slaveholders—and even those who did not own slaves—were doing whatever they could to justify and defend slavery. But they were not alone in insisting that blacks were not the equals of whites and should not be treated as such. After all, Louis Agassiz, who was deeply committed to the inferiority of blacks, was born in Switzerland and taught at Harvard University. Francis Lieber, the German-born political theorist, attributed the growth of republican institutions to the superior qualities of what he called "the Anglican race." Lydia Maria Child, who was a vigorous proponent of emancipation, believed that the races of mankind were different, spiritually as well as physically. Samuel Joseph May, Unitarian minister and abolitionist, ventured the opinion that not one in a hundred of the thirty thousand ministers in the United States differed with the prevailing view of blacks, openly condemned slavery, or "lifted a finger" to protect a fugitive slave. Thus, long before the Civil War, a wide variety of Americans—abolitionists, scientists, clergy, and slaveholders, Southern and Northern—subscribed to a doctrine of racial differences that justified slavery and precluded equal treatment.

The view of racial differences could lead to some strange positions on the part of those who held it. It could lead to what George Frederickson has called "romantic racialism" that could cause Orville Dewey, the New York Unitarian minister, to admire the childlike inferiority of the Negro. The traits of docility, affection, and patience spared the Negro from the rough, fierce energies that adversely affected the Christian character of so many Northern whites. William Ellery Channing in 1835 said it was these traits that made it possible for blacks to escape "the moral degradation that seemed an inevitable consequence of their condition." Robert Dale Owen, the utopian reformer, thought these traits, together with the genial spirit of blacks, would make themselves felt "as an element of improvement in the national character." Blacks, still in slavery and still degraded, were supposed to get much consolation from the fact that the geniality which sustained them in slavery would, somehow, have a salutary effect on the national character.

Not all white Northerners who saw differences between blacks and whites were romantic racialists, however. In many a Northern community any move to provide educational opportunities for blacks or any other facilities which would suggest equality was resisted on the ground that such moves were not only unseemly but futile. In 1831 a New Haven town meeting opposed the establishment of a college for blacks in that community by a vote of seven hundred to four. "What possible good can arise from giving them a collegiate education," the *New York Courier and Enquirer* asked. "Will it give them that equality which exists among white men? Certainly not. The very leaders who open their purses for such objects will not allow a learned Negro to sit at their tables or marry their daughter."

Several years later, when Prudence Crandall, a young white teacher, admitted a black girl to her school in Canterbury, Connecticut, the white parents withdrew their daughters. And when she then established a school for Negro girls, harassment by white citizens took the form of shops refusing provisions, hoodlums filling the school's well with manure, and the village physician refusing to treat the black pupils. Finally, the *coup de grace* was administered by the state legislature which passed a law forbidding the establishment of any school for the instruction of "colored persons who are not inhabitants of this state."

Racial hostility in the North and the refusal of whites to permit blacks to participate in the life of the community on any basis approaching equality created a situation almost as bleak there as in the slave-ridden South. "Why should I strive hard to acquire all the constituents of a man if the prevailing genius of the land admit me not as such," asked the valedictorian of the graduating class at a Negro school in 1819. White mechanics would not work with him, and no employer would have him in his office. "Drudgery and servitude are my prospective portion. Can you be surprised at my discouragement?" He could have added that competition with hostile immigrants frequently degenerated into violence, and he could not even be certain of securing menial jobs or decent housing, while his generally degraded position was regarded by many as a living monument to the folly of the abolitionists.

But the position of the abolitionists themselves on the matter of racial equality was, at best, ambivalent. To be sure, they were quite aware of the fact that free Negroes and slaves shared a similar plight. Gerrit Smith declared that Northern laws, institutions, and customs rendered the "freedom of the colored people but an empty name—but the debasing mockery of true freedom." Many abolitionists, nevertheless, were disinclined to enter into complete fellowship with free blacks on the basis of equality. On the pretense that they must respect the feelings, even the prejudices of their opponents, some abolitionists wanted to bar blacks from their organizations and to have no social contact with them. "We ought never to have permitted our colored brethren to unite with us in our associations," said William Ellery Channing, the father of the Unitarian Church.

In words reminiscent of the concessions made to slaveholders at the Constitutional Convention of 1787, Lewis Tappan said that on the "ticklish point" of mixing with people of color in public, in order to "prevent disunion" he yielded to those who said the time was not ripe. Some abolitionists insisted, of course, that refusing to receive blacks into the societies working to end slavery or to mix with them as equals was rank hypocrisy. Thus, the question of what to do with respect to their own race relations plagued the abolitionists right down to the Civil War. This was a clear indication of how deeply ingrained in American life was the notion that Negroes should not be treated as equals.

If antebellum social activists had difficulty with the problem of racial equality, there were scarcely any politicians who did. William H. Seward, whom many regarded as the leading candidate for the Republican presidential nomination in 1860, regarded Negroes as incapable of assimilation. They were, in his words, "a pitiful exotic unnecessarily transplanted into our fields." Salmon P. Chase, the militant free-soil Senator from Ohio, told Frederick

Douglass that he "looked forward to the separation of the races" since blacks and whites were adapted to different latitudes and countries. Abraham Lincoln, who would achieve the goal in 1860 to which both Seward and Chase aspired, was more unequivocal. In 1858, in the debates with Stephen A. Douglas, Lincoln saw the differences between the two races as quite real and insurmountable. "There is a physical difference between the two races," he said, "which . . . will probably forever forbid their living together on a footing of perfect equality." And he was frank to say it was his firm opinion that the black man was not his equal in "intellectual and moral endowments."

Thus, three of the leading antislavery political leaders in mid-nineteenth-century America held the view that blacks and whites were so different and that whites were so clearly superior to blacks that they could not possibly live together in an egalitarian society. And as the nation was plunged into a war to save itself and subsequently to abolish slavery, neither the leaders nor the citizenry were prepared to face the far-reaching social, economic, and political implications in the emergence of four million persons from slavery to freedom.

The nation's only experience in the area had been with free blacks; and nowhere, not even in the North, had this group, numbering a half million in 1860, been treated as equals. Illinois, Indiana, Iowa, and Oregon not only disfranchised free Negroes but barred their further entry. In states where they did vote, they suffered other disabilities such as exclusion from the militia or having no educational opportunities. Some leaders such as Martin R. Delany, Henry Highland Garnet, and Samuel Ringgold Ward seriously considered expatriation. In 1860, a few days before the election, an anti-Republican parade in New York City featured banners bearing such slogans as "No Negro Equality" and "Free Love, Free Niggers, and Free Women." As the nation was preparing to fight to save itself and even to end slavery, it was making no preparation to incorporate free Negroes and emancipated slaves into the fellowship of equal American citizenship. The old order had not changed.

In the final months of the war President Lincoln was apparently giving considerable thought to how the old order could be changed. Even in the final draft of the Emancipation Proclamation he dropped all reference to the plan to colonize blacks that he had earlier explored and had even included in the preliminary proclamation. He had either concluded that blacks were here to stay regardless of his own desires or that as pioneers in the settlement and as fighters for union, blacks had a right to remain in this country as much as anyone else. He also began to think seriously about what should be done for Negroes to secure their rights and protect them in the exercise of those rights. In 1864, in a letter to a friend, he said, "I cannot see, if universal amnesty is granted, how, under the circumstances, I can avoid exacting universal suffrage or, at least, suffrage on the basis of intelligence and military service." Later, Lincoln said he hoped that the various states would take steps "by which the two races could gradually live themselves out of their old relation to each other and both come out better prepared for the new."

It appeared that the President was now prepared to implement a view, radical for its time, he had expressed two decades earlier. In 1846 he had said, "We feel . . . that all legal distinctions between individuals of the same community, founded in any such circumstances on color, origin, and the like, are hostile to the genius of our institutions, and incompatible with the true history of American liberty." It was as though the war had worked some almost mystically transforming influence on Lincoln. Few had suffered during those war years more than Abraham Lincoln; and no leader's views and plans for the future had undergone such profound changes. No one appreciated more than Lincoln that government should be the instrument for effecting a change from the old order to the new.

Lincoln had no opportunity to implement his views; and there was no one else even remotely prepared to attempt to do so. A former slaveholder and a peculiarly Negrophobic vice-president succeeded Lincoln in 1865. Meanwhile, former slaveholders were in firm control of virtually every state government in the former Confederacy. Negro inequality was written into every constitution in the Southern states, and black codes, barely distinguishable in many respects from the old slave codes, had become law before the end of 1865. To be sure, many of these laws were repealed during the years 1867–77 when Congress wielded some power and when blacks and their white allies attempted to reverse the tide in some of the Southern states. But the principle of racial inequality had been dramatically reasserted just as the smoldering embers of a fiery Civil War died out; and even during the period of so-called Radical Reconstruction that principle was never successfully challenged.

In the last four decades of the nineteenth century, nothing occurred in the North to challenge the principle of racial inequality. The abolitionists who survived the war congratulated themselves that there was no more slavery, and most of them were quite ready to dissolve their various organizations that now seemed redundant. The rejoicing was premature, even about emancipation, for several Southern states felt disinclined to renounce slavery in the constitutions they were writing in 1865. Meanwhile, as John and LaWanda Cox have reminded us, the Thirteenth Amendment to end slavery passed the House of Representatives with just two votes to spare, and there is a very real likelihood that it would not have passed without the pressure of President Lincoln and the powerful lobbying by Secretary of State Seward. When the Amendment reached the Southern states for ratification, they were willing to recognize that slavery was dead, but they were not willing to ratify a constitutional provision that gave to Congress the power of enforcement. They wanted to permit nothing that would interfere with their plan to exercise full control over the freedmen and keep them in a subordinate position.

Racial equality could not be achieved during Reconstruction by piecemeal actions of the several states, North and South. In the former Confederate states, the so-called reconstructed governments did not establish racial equality, for the shaky coalition of Northern whites living in the South, loyal Southern whites, and newly enfranchised Negroes could not agree on programs to achieve and implement such a goal. Even if they had reached agreement, the powerful disfranchised whites and terrorist groups like the Ku Klux Klan would have seen to it that they were never carried out. Except among Negroes, many of whom were weak, inexperienced, and unorganized, there was no deep commitment to racial equality. As Francis Cardoza, a Negro leader in South Carolina declared in 1867, "We bear no enmity to any, but we are determined to secure our rights, and by the eternal vigilance that is the price of liberty, with God's blessing, we hope we shall." If white Southerners were at all concerned about black Southerners moving significantly on the road to equality, they need not have been; for the position of freedmen in the postwar South was scarcely better than that of free blacks in the antebellum period.

The long, dreary debates over what to include in the Fourteenth Amendment and how to define equality indicated that Congress was no better prepared to extend equality to blacks than it was to guarantee their freedom. They were clearly citizens, of course, if they were "born or naturalized in the United States," but the injunction not to deprive persons of their life, liberty, or property or deny them equal protection of the laws was against the states, not the federal government. When the Amendment was before the states, the bitterness of the debates, marked among other bizarre incidents by Ohio and New Jersey withdrawing their ratification, clearly shows the range of feeling on racial equality from ambivalence to opposition. And when Congress enacted a civil rights law, after debating it for five years, to give meaning to the equal protection clause, the Republican floor manager for the bill was asked if it was intended to permit Negroes to patronize saloons frequented by whites. He said definitely not; after all, there should be some places left where whites would not be annoyed by the presence of blacks!

The question was academic, anyway, for the federal government never enforced the law; and in 1883 the Supreme Court struck it down on the ground that the Fourteenth Amendment did not authorize the Congress to take action to protect the rights of black people. The Court had taken a similar position in outlawing congressional legislation to protect the voting rights of blacks that presumably had been guaranteed by the Fifteenth Amendment.

Thus, the Reconstruction years were marked by half-hearted, light-hearted, inconclusive steps taken by the state and federal governments to introduce a semblance of racial equality in America. The feeble effort was an abject failure. There was no shame in the South as terror struck the black community, bringing whippings, arson, and murder in its wake. There was no shame in the North where, answering President Grant's plea, "Let us have peace," the acquiescence with the South's arrogation of the responsibility for the black man's subjugation was all but complete. The price of liberty and equality was, as Cardoza has said, eternal vigilance. But the price of peace was a surrender to the principles of racial inequality. An uneasy racial peace settled over the South and North, as the old order of racial degradation, now buttressed by Supreme Court decisions and executive and legislative indifference and inactivity, continued to prevail.

In the final quarter of the nineteenth century and the early years of the twentieth century the position of the Negro reached what Rayford W. Logan has called the nadir. Those were the years, Logan said, when the betrayal of the Negro was complete. It began with the federal government's abandonment of its feeble attempt to protect the rights of black people, and it ended with the bloody race riots in a dozen American cities following the close of World War I. The intervening years produced the most remarkable and incredible display of racial arrogance, bigotry, and inequality this country had ever witnessed. This was not the work of newly arrived immigrants, although many of them joined in, if for no other reason than to deflect attention from themselves. It was the work of some of the oldest and most respected elements of society. In the end, the dream of racial equality was a complete shambles; and the old order of white racial superiority was more deeply entrenched than ever.

Social Darwinism, the application to society of the doctrine of the struggle for existence and the survival of the fittest, was a highly respectable explanation for the failure of blacks to achieve equality in American life. One of its most influential and distinguished proponents, Professor William Graham Sumner of Yale University, said that nothing was more certain than that "inequality is the law of life." Whether the black man was the equal of a white man was not an essential question. "Since the South considered the Negro to be inferior, the only practical question was how to deal with that opinion." The doctrine of evolution, "instead of supporting the natural equality of man would give a demonstration of their inequality," he said. The Sumner doctrine became a prevailing view, shared by educators, politicians, and industrialists. For them it was a satisfactory and convenient explanation for any degradation that blacks experienced in their struggle for survival. What was even more to the point, there was nothing that anyone, including the agents of government, could do about it. For, as

Sumner insisted in a statement that would become famous in his time and infamous in later generations, "stateways cannot change folkways."

To make certain Negro Americans would never be accorded equality, the most respectable magazines and newspapers of the country launched a frontal assault on any and all suggestions that blacks were even worthy of citizenship and the equal protection of the laws. They were congenitally criminal, the *North American Review* argued in 1884. They were notorious liars, Thomas Nelson Page, the Virginia patrician, insisted in 1892. They were a "race alien, animal, half savage" a writer in *Harper's Magazine* claimed in 1887. They were improvident, emotional, gossipy, kind-hearted, high-tempered, vain, dishonest, and idle, asserted an author in the same magazine a few years earlier. Such views led many prominent Americans to conclude that Afro-Americans, with their numerous deficiencies and disqualifications for equality, were truly the white man's burden and that Southern leaders had been correct in their assessment of the Negro's not being worthy of citizenship.

Small wonder that there were few voices raised anywhere against the far-reaching program looking to the degradation and humiliation of blacks everywhere. In 1883, when the Supreme Court declared unconstitutional the Civil Rights Act of 1875, the decision was hailed throughout the land as just in every respect. A Philadelphia editor said that the Negro people should accept the decision "with patience and strive by self-improvement and good citizenship" to win the respect of whites. There was no loud outcry against the disfranchisement of blacks by the Southern state constitutions between 1890 and 1905. To be sure, Mississippi, South Carolina, and the other disfranchising states received some gentle raps on the knuckles, but the indiscriminate and wholesale withdrawal of the franchise from hundreds of thousands of blacks was not viewed in Washington or elsewhere as the destruction of democratic institutions.

When the Southern states, encouraged by the separate but equal doctrine set forth in *Plessy* v. *Ferguson* in 1896, began to enact additional legislation to segregate the races, most white Americans registered little objection. And no wonder. The separate railroad car in Tennessee was matched by customary if not legal separation of the races in the New York theater. The separate telephone booths for blacks and whites in Oklahoma had their rough counterpart in the racially segregated units of the United States Army. It was a cruel concept of separate but equal that permitted South Carolina to expend eight dollars on the education of a white child to every dollar spent on a black child. It was equally cruel to shunt a black child and his family into New York's Harlem, or into Philadelphia's Seventh Ward, or into Chicago's South Side, where the view of the glaring inequities was somewhat mitigated by their very isolation. By this time, moreover, the bus was being invented and with it the notorious invention of busing schoolchildren in order to maintain segregated schools. And when white children were transported for miles past black schools so that they could attend white schools, not one word of opposition was uttered against such forced busing.

In 1902 William E. B. Du Bois said that the problem of the twentieth century would be the problem of the color line. As far back as 1875 the Negro members of Congress, speaking in favor of the Civil Rights Bill, had intimated as much. In 1883, T. Thomas Fortune, the fiery editor of the New York *Age*, doubted that his people would ever achieve equality in the United States. Even Booker T. Washington, in accepting, at least temporarily, a subordinate place for Negroes in American life, had to look far into the distant future to discover any fulfillment of the optimism he expressed in his celebrated Atlanta speech in 1895. Du Bois succinctly stated what all of them saw when he said, "despite compromise, war, and struggle, the Negro is not free. . . . And there in the King's Highway sat and sits a figure veiled and bowed, by which the traveller's footsteps hasten as they go. On the tainted air broods fear. Three centuries' thought has been the raising and unveiling of that bowed human heart, and now behold a new century for the duty and the deed."

With all his prescience Du Bois could hardly have known how intractable was the problem of race in America or how utterly and deeply committed so many Americans were to the principle of racial inequality. He knew of the lynchings in the backwoods of the South; but he did not know that a distinguished professor at Harvard had said that if a black student won a certain coveted prize, they would have to forgo the traditional dinner honoring the winner. He knew that a hundred legal and constitutional devices had been employed to eliminate Negroes from politics, but he did not know that the President of the United States, Theodore Roosevelt, had written a friend that "as a race, and in the mass, the blacks are altogether inferior to the whites." Had he known that people at the very apex of American political and intellectual life had such low opinions of blacks, he might well have been moved to say that the problem of the *twenty-first* century would be the problem of the color line.

The problem was rendered even more complex and difficult, if such was possible, by the new perspective afforded by the new American imperialism. Whether a burgeoning racism helped to stimulate America's imperialistic impulse or acted as a deterrent, there can be no doubt that once an American empire was acquired the attitudes toward backward peoples in the empire and toward so-called backward Negroes at home reinforced each other. The elevation of the Negro was the "white man's burden here, as it is elsewhere in the world today," said the Reverend W. A. Guerry of the University of the South. The experience with imperialism, moreover, was modifying certain older concepts of democracy, "correcting some of our doctrinaire conceptions as to the natural equality of men," as one observer put it. This is what George Frederickson has called "accommodationist racism," since it sees the black future "in terms of a permanent and allegedly benevolent domestic colonialism." For persons who viewed the matter in this light, their "programs of moral uplift, industrial training, and racial integrity really meant, therefore, that they regarded the American black population not as an incorrigible menace to white civilization, but as a useful and quiescent internal colony."

One cannot view the United States in the first two decades of the twentieth century without realizing that the dream of racial justice and equality had turned into a hideous nightmare; twelve hundred Negroes lynched in the decade ending in 1908—some for insolence, for not stepping aside for whites, or for disputes over wages; eight major and many minor race riots during the same period, engendering even greater antipathies in such places as Atlanta, Georgia, Brownsville, Texas, and Springfield, Illinois; an entire battalion of Negro soldiers dismissed by the President of the United States without a hearing and without honor for allegedly participating in a riot. It would take all the energy and resources of the newly organized interracial National Association for the Advancement of Colored People merely to keep the very idea of racial equality alive and to remind federal officials that they had taken an oath to uphold the Constitution, including the Thirteenth, Fourteenth, and Fifteenth Amendments.

But the idea of racial equality receded even more from public awareness with the accession to the presidency of Woodrow Wilson. During the campaign in 1912 Wilson said he wished to see "justice done to the colored people in every matter; and not mere grudging justice, but justice executed with liberality and cordial good feeling." Later, as blacks began to desert the Republican party and support this bright new face on the national scene, Wilson said he wanted to "assure them that should I become President of the United States they may count upon me for absolute fair dealing, for everything by which I could assist in advancing the interests of their race in the United States." His was, at best, a curious view of justice and a perverted notion of what would advance the interests of Negroes in the United States. Within a few months after he took office Wilson, by executive order, had segregated black and white federal employees in eating and rest room facilities and had begun, wherever possible, to phase blacks out of the civil service. Within a short while he lent the prestige of his position to a much publicized showing in the White House of the motion picture, "Birth of a Nation," which even in 1976 was the one document most responsible for the distorted view of the role of blacks during the era of Reconstruction.

Although he certainly acquiesced in the country's racial military policy, Woodrow Wilson did not make that policy. Segregation and discrimination in the armed forces of the United States were as old as the armed forces themselves. Segregation in the standing army had been formally institutionalized just after the Civil War, with the establishment of two regiments of infantry and two of cavalry with black enlisted men staffed largely with white officers. Black men had always been excluded from the marines and from the navy except as menials; and from military aviation until World War II. And there had never been more than a very few black officers until the government established a segregated officer school in 1917.

Nor had anything changed very much as far as American inconsistency in matters of race was concerned. As Edmund Morgan has pointed out, the nation purchased its political independence in the eighteenth century with slave labor. In the nineteenth century it fought to save itself and to abolish slavery, but at the same time declined to give freedmen the political and economic tools with which to gain full and equal citizenship. Now, in the twentieth century the nation sent a segregated army to Europe to save the world for democracy; and its instructions to the French into whose military forces the Negro American soldiers were to be integrated was not to treat the Negroes as equals. Care must be taken, said the United States government document, *Secret Information concerning Black Troops*, to maintain complete separation of blacks and whites, lest blacks assault and rape French women. It would be most unfortunate, it warned the French officers, if they associated with Negro officers or had any contact with them outside the requirements of military service.

It was not without a touch of irony that as the white Americans instructed the French about black Americans, the German enemy was instructing black Americans about white Americans. Blacks should not be deluded into thinking that they were fighting for humanity and democracy. "What is Democracy?" the Germans asked. "Personal freedom, all citizens enjoying the same rights socially and before the law. Do you enjoy the same rights as the white people do in America, the land of Freedom and Democracy, or are you rather not treated over there as second-class citizens?" Black soldiers knew the answers to the questions, for they had asked them long before the Germans had. They had fought segregation in the army, had fought white civilians who had taunted and insulted them even as they wore the uniform of their country, had been shunted aside by their own country and dumped into the the hands of French officers whom they neither knew nor understood. They could tell the Germans much about what it meant to be second-class citizens.

That is what the American military establishment feared, and that is what white civilian America feared. If black American soldiers returned to the United States embittered and aggressive, a holocaust of untold proportions might visit the land. Jefferson had mentioned that possibility more than a century earlier; and the colonizationists had foreseen it a half-century later. As the black soldiers returned to savor the democracy for which they had fought in the Argonne and on the Moselle, they soon learned that during their absence racial justice and equality had once again receded from view. Some Negroes were lynched or burned alive while still in uniform. A young Negro swimmer floated across the racial line of demarcation in Lake Michigan, setting off a four-day anti-black riot in Chicago that cost the lives of thirty-eight people. The rumor of blacks assaulting white women in Washington threw the nation's capital into three days of frenzied rioting, looting, and burning. Up and down the country—in East St. Louis, Illinois; Knoxville, Tennessee; Omaha, Nebraska; Elaine, Arkansas; Longview, Texas—the response to any bid for political or economic equality of the races was violence.

What had been accomplished in the previous century in the area of racial equality? The only really honest answer must be very little indeed. The century had begun with a strong assertion that the union could be preserved only if slavery were permitted to flourish. With that accomplished there ensued a campaign, more successful than its protagonists could have dreamed, to justify racial inequality on the basis of science, religion, economics, and sociology. It was so successful, in fact, that the emancipation of the slaves had no discernible effect on the movement for racial equality. And the poison of racism permeated American thought and American policy so thoroughly that neither war nor peace nor pestilence nor famine could have created a climate favorable to racial equality. It was not merely that the old order had not changed. It was that the old order had become reinvigorated by a renewed commitment on the part of a frightening majority of white Americans to a position that did not tolerate even the advocacy of racial equality. If this was a betrayal of the early American dream, they seemed willing to make the most of it.

A review of the struggle for and against racial equality in the nineteenth century provides a necessary context for understanding the persistence and the pervasiveness of the problem as we move into the last quarter of the twentieth century. Louis Agassiz and Samuel Cartwright did what they could to rationalize inequality in the nineteenth century, but the neo-Klansmen and the White Citizens Councils and the dozens of groups and movements opposed to racial equality in recent times have sought to link themselves with those earlier sages of racial bigotry and thus establish and emphasize the validity and continuity of the program to exclude black Americans from the enjoyment of equality. David Walker, in his *Appeal* of 1829, sought to perform the task for his progeny by striking a blow for equality. But Martin Luther King had to do it all over again as though David Walker had never lived. The repression and violence that characterized the successful drive to maintain the inequalities of the past have their counterpart in the quiet, subtle, but effective efforts of today to maintain a measurable distance between whites who enjoy equality and blacks who do not.

Even now as we witness significant and substantial moves toward equality, the tendency toward self-congratulation stimulates complacency and in-difference. And this in turn creates a resistance to the achievement of complete equality. We point with pride to the election of one black man to public office or the appointment of one black woman to a position of responsibility in the private sector. That is hardly an expiation for all that has happened to deny equality of blacks for three hundred years, but we are tempted to believe that it is. Racial violence continues to stalk the land. Inequalities of infinite varieties and complexities persist. Racial injustice in housing, employment, and education pervades the nation. Their linkage to the sins of our fathers of the eighteenth and nineteenth centuries is clear. If they stumbled, groped, and fell—for whatever reasons—that was their misfortune, but it should not be ours.

> We shall not always plant while others reap
> The golden increment of bursting fruit,
> Not always countenance, abject and mute,
> That lesser men should hold their brothers cheap;
> Not everlastingly while others sleep
> Shall we beguile their limbs with mellow flute,
> Not always bend to some more subtle brute;
> We were not made eternally to weep.

> The night whose sable breast relieves the stark
> White stars is no less lovely being dark,
> And there are buds that cannot bloom at all
> In light, but crumple, piteous, and fall;
> So in the dark we hide the heart that bleeds.
> And wait, and tend our agonizing needs.

three

Equality Indivisible

Almost from the beginning of their national history, Americans have been relentless, at times ruthless, in their pursuit of equality. The notion prevailed among them that any mark of superiority, however legitimate, somehow suggested privilege; and that would not be tolerated in a society striving to become democratic. This was a principal reason for abolishing the English law of primogeniture and entail in the late eighteenth century. In most states no son who inherited his father's estate had any right to be placed at an advantage over his siblings. Thus, it seemed no more than right that descendants should share equally the inheritance from their father.

Likewise, a major reason for the establishment of the common school was to make certain that private wealth did not place some children at an advantage over others in the acquisition of knowledge. Americans held firm to the view that in a democratic society there should be no aristocracy of talent, especially if it resulted from the enjoyment of special privileges. Only in the South was privilege acceptable, and even there some critics carried on a running attack against it.

The widespread views favoring equality, however estimable, were flawed by conditions and qualifications that seriously undermined the very principle of equality itself. The old laws of inheritance were not meant to apply to persons of African descent, and the same held true for the new laws of inheritance that sought to establish equality. Most blacks—slaves, that is—down to the middle of the nineteenth century could not legally own property of any kind and consequently could not inherit or transmit it. Free Negroes were begrudgingly conceded the right to own property, but their own status was at all times so precarious that the ownership of property was frequently more of a burden than an asset. It could be taken from them on the slightest pretext or provocation; and the task of proving ownership in a hostile or indifferent court was greater than most of them could successfully undertake. The new property laws designed to establish greater equality were not meant for them, and they derived little if any benefit from these legal innovations.

Likewise, the idea of a common school education in the United States was conceived and promoted for white children who, presumably, would undergo a leavening experience that would give them a sense of equality even among the more privileged. Black children, however, were denied such an opportunity because it was assumed that they were incapable of benefiting from such an experience and because white society had defined for them an inferior role in which education was really not necessary anyway.

Thus, they were officially denied every opportunity for an education in the slave states, while in the free states they were largely excluded from the schools for whites and were given only that training deemed suitable for their inferior status. Indeed, in many places in the North their exclusion from educational opportunities was as complete as it was in the South.

As one views the problems of racial equality over the last two or three centuries, it becomes clear that a prime concern of the policy makers was to create distinctions between those who were regarded as equals and those who were not. To put it another way, many of the policy makers were committed to the idea that it was entirely possible to divide equality. The attempt to do so—that is, to accord complete equality of opportunity, condition, or circumstance to some while withholding it from others— would become not only one of the major preoccupations of Americans in the twentieth century but a major policy problem at every level of American society and government. The story as well as the problem of racial equality in twentieth-century America is essentially the story of the struggle to divide a privilege or a right whose indivisibility would become more and more apparent.

By the end of World War I it appeared that the formula for dividing equality in such a way that some enjoyed it while others did not was approaching perfection. And the basis for division was primarily race. In the political sphere the practice of excluding Negroes from the franchise had become a fine art as well as a nearly perfected practice in political science. The white Democratic primary prevailed in every Southern state, thus nullifying the Negro vote in most places and rendering it ineffective where it existed at all. It did not matter that the Fifteenth Amendment had been a part of the Constitution for fifty years or that the United States Supreme Court in the 1915 decision involving the grandfather clause had warned states about attempting to circumvent the constitutional guarantee of voting rights. The white primary, which was tantamount to an election in the Southern states where more than eighty per cent of black Americans lived in 1920, reduced them to a status of abject political inferiority while conferring on whites, all whites, a euphoric condition of complete political equality.

In the area of making a living the situation was similar. The reaction against blacks' continuing to enjoy the few economic gains they had made during the war was strong. Those who remained in the South were saddled with a host of economic burdens ranging from the boll weevil, which did not discriminate between black and white farms, to the crop lien system to virtual exclusion from the new industries. In the North, to which several hundred thousand had migrated during the war years, the situation was scarcely better. The warm welcome that greeted blacks as they began to relieve the labor shortage in Northern industries during the war was not sustained in the postwar years. Equal employment opportunity was as alien as the Bolshevik mottoes; and if blacks persisted in demanding jobs, they were considered to be as un-American as the Bolsheviks themselves. One of the first projects of the new Federal Bureau of Investigation was to maintain surveillance over the National Urban League that was engaged in the 1920s in the highly suspicious work of trying to find jobs for unemployed Negro laborers. As the pawns of management, black workers had been used to break the strikes of the unions from which they had been excluded. And when the strikes were over, the black workers lost their attractiveness to the employer, who then proceeded to replace them with white laborers. As Sterling Spero and Abram Harris observed, where there were employment opportunities they were not equal; and the greatest inequality was where there was no employment at all because of race.

Racial segregation and discrimination in education were a hallmark of the years following World War I. No Southern state made any effort to equalize educational opportunities for black and white children. Without the aid to Negro schools provided by Northern philanthropy, even as late as the 1920s, the situation would have been even more deplorable. Mississippi Senator James K. Vardaman had warned before the war that what the North was sending South was not money but dynamite. "This education is ruining our Negroes. They're demanding equality." Vardaman was given to excessive statements, and this was no exception. But it was true that since white Southerners had no intention of providing equal educational opportunities for blacks and whites, the Northerners might well ruin their game plan.

Meanwhile, white Northerners who had insisted on their own commitment to equality became disturbed over the number of blacks moving into their midst. It was one thing for Northern whites to concede equality for all blacks in the South or to a few hundred in the North. It was quite another thing for them to concede equality to the many thousands of blacks who were taking up permanent residence in the North. White leaders in the North were obviously alarmed and they did not conceal their desire to establish and maintain segregated schools in communities where the black population was large. In Chicago a white member of the Board of Education went so far as to suggest racially separate schools. "How in your opinion," he asked several prominent Negroes, "should a separation movement, if under any circumstances it is wise, be begun?" One Negro leader replied that he was astonished and insulted, while the editor of the black Chicago *Defender* advised those who had received the letter to ignore it. Despite these reactions, with the emergence of the black ghetto in one city after another, segregated and unequal education on the basis of race became easy to maintain. And what was true of employment and education was true of housing, social services, public accommodations, and virtually every area of human activity where, under normal circumstances, members of the two races would have made contact with each other.

The origin of the tragic situation among the urban poor blacks today can be traced to the conditions that prevailed in the years following World War I and, later, World War II. Herded into ghettoes without employment, usually because of race, and consequently without the means of providing for their families, they were overcome by frustration, disillusionment, and despair. Housing that was substandard or inadequate to begin with became more run down under the weight of overcrowding. With nothing to enrich their lives, many engaged in petty crimes and shady activities to make a few dollars as well as to lift the pall of boredom. Lacking the supervision of mothers who, more often than fathers, found some employment and lacking the supervision of fathers who found the role of homemaker distasteful, children drifted into truancy and delinquency. The corner grocer, charging exorbitant prices for goods on credit, was as cruel in his demands as the landlord in the South had been when he operated the commissary for sharecroppers. Without opportunities of some kind there was no equality of any kind. In creating and perpetuating a black ghetto where such conditions prevailed, the Northern city was setting a time bomb whose explosion would be as damaging as it would be inevitable.

The division of a society into groups whose eligibility to enjoy the accepted norms of equality was based on race would not be as easy to maintain in the future as it had been in the past. Already, in the 1920s, patterns of aggression as well as resistance were emerging on the battleground of racial equality that would be a part of the picture for the ensuing fifty years. When Dr. A. L. Nixon, the black dentist in El Paso, Texas, brought suit in 1927 to challenge the white primary there, he began the drive to achieve political equality for blacks. The drive would be punctuated by court cases that put white primary officials on the run in all states where blacks were excluded. It would tax the ingenuity and creativity of those officials until they were finally brought to bay in 1947. It would culminate in the Voting Rights Act of 1965 and the election of thousands of blacks to public office in the decade that followed.

The step that Dr. Nixon took was more than a challenge to a respected and venerated practice of race orthodoxy in the South. It was a signal to white Americans, North and South, that there were educated, articulate, and courageous black Americans who were no longer willing to accept the inequality that by this time had become as American as apple pie or major league baseball. Even in the complex and difficult field of economic life, they showed a remarkable determination to fight for racial equality. The New Negro, said A. Philip Randolph in his magazine *The Messenger*, would not be "lulled into a false sense of security with political spoils and patronage." He must have the full product of his toil that was being consistently denied him by management and white organized labor. And he stood for "absolute social equality, education, physical action in self-defense, and freedom of speech, press, and assembly." If they could not even aspire to these modest goals that would mark them as equals in the American system, then they would embrace more radical approaches, such as socialism as advocated by the Friends of Negro Freedom or even Black Zionism as advocated by Marcus Garvey.

But it was not radicalism that so many blacks embraced unless it was the radicalism of equal protection of the laws, which was guaranteed by the Constitution but was neither honored nor enforced. This was the radicalism of Ossian H. Sweet, the Negro physician in Detroit who together with friends had to protect his newly purchased home from the assault of a white mob in 1925. When he was indicted for murder for killing a member of the mob as it charged toward the entrance of his home, the question was whether the preservation of an "ethnic treasure" or "ethnic purity" was more important than the protection of one's life and property that the police had declined to protect. The jury thought it was not, and Dr. Sweet was exonerated.

Nor was it an alien radicalism that prompted blacks in New York, St. Louis, Cleveland, and Chicago to seek employment in the business establishments in the black ghetto. The Jobs-for-Negroes movement in St. Louis and the Citizens' League for

Fair Play in New York City had the modest objective of securing employment for Negroes in neighborhood businesses that they patronized but from employment in which they were systematically excluded. Harlem street corners, where blacks harangued their listeners concerning the injustice of whites refusing to hire black workers, were reminiscent of London's Hyde Park. But they were also reminiscent of Boston Commons in the Revolutionary Era or Seneca Falls, New York, in the mid-nineteenth-century struggle for women's rights. It was in the best American tradition, but the universality of the struggle against inequality could hardly be denied.

Inequality in the administration of justice and the enforcement of the laws was apparent to any who cared to look. In 1921 a Negro was burned to death over a slow fire at Nodena, Arkansas. In the following year a mob, including women and children, slowly roasted a black man in Hubbard, Texas, while jabbing sticks into his mouth, nose, and eyes. Incidents like these caused William Pickens to describe the South as "The American Congo." After being forbidden by two white policemen with drawn guns to defend himself when a white man struck him, a young Houston Negro asked the Attorney General of the United States "just what is a negro worth here in Houston, as he is counted no more than a stray dog." In 1927 Nick Childs, black editor of the Topeka *Plaindealer*, told President Coolidge he could not see "how a President of the United

States can sit idly by and see his living subjects burned to death by a degenerated class of evil doers." The reply from Washington was always the same. The Department of Justice even had a form letter it sent to any blacks pleading for protection. It said, "The Department ... regrets to advise you that it would have no authority to take any action with reference to the matter to which you refer inasmuch as the State ... possesses exclusive jurisdiction in the premises."

The inequities were nowhere more glaring than in the determination to exclude Negroes from a fair share of relief and employment during the depression and New Deal years. It took a special brand of inhumanity to exclude hungry blacks from soup kitchens operated by religious and charitable groups; but white Americans showed they possessed that special brand of inhumanity. "Its awful bad to wait for someone who does not care to give you food," one Alabama black complained in 1934. In the same year another Southern Negro reported that when his son went to sign up for relief work, a group of whites knocked him down, chased him with a bulldog, and threatened to murder him if he attempted again to secure relief.

In the early programs of public assistance there was, in some places, as much as a six-dollar differential in the monthly aid given to white and black families. This was about the time that Robert Weaver, a black New Deal economist, complained bitterly that wage differentials based on race rather than training, experience, or efficiency threatened to destroy not only the New Deal recovery program but any hope of having a really egalitarian labor movement in the United States. Despite the efforts of some New Deal administrators to establish racial equality in relief and employment, neither the Congress nor the President was willing to support such lofty goals. Indeed, when the Farm Security Administration began to move toward a policy of racial equality, powerful members of Congress insisted that Communists were controlling its program. Consequently, they proceeded to destroy it by cutting off its appropriations.

The dilatoriness of the federal government in the matter of racial equality was dramatically underscored during World War II. Industries with huge government contracts were frank to say that they did not practice equal employment and had no intention of doing so. The President would make no move to act on behalf of racial equality in employment until A. Philip Randolph and Walter White threatened to bring 100,000 Negroes to Washington to dramatize the inequalities in both the public and private sectors. And the committee established by the President to oversee fair employment had neither sufficient legal powers nor adequate government support to achieve fair employment even in those industries where government contracts were involved. Twenty years after the establishment of the first Presidential Committee on Fair Employment, the United States Commission on Civil Rights concluded that such committees had had little effect on traditional patterns of Negro employment.

Since World War II was a struggle against a particularly obnoxious brand of racism as well as a most reprehensible form of totalitarianism, consistency as well as sensitivity to the issues seemed to require the United States to pursue a policy of racial equality in its fight against Nazism. But the United States was neither consistent nor sensitive to the larger issues of the war as they related to the domestic scene. The United States Army remained segregated, with the inevitable inferior facilities and second-class status for black soldiers. At long last the Air Force, the Navy, and the Marines were opened to blacks but on a segregated basis. One would be hard pressed to find a more ridiculous posture from which to fight the Nazi racists than to point to the Jim Crow officer school for black pilots at Tuskegee, where the contact with the United States Air Force was barely discernible. Even as the move began, late in the war, to integrate the armed services on a limited basis, racial equality seemed a far-off goal to which Americans moved haltingly and even indifferently.

It was neither Hitler nor Mussolini that began to move the United States from the old order of segregation, discrimination, and racial inequality in general. Rather, it was the outrage of blacks and some whites at the hypocrisy of the American position in the war. The nation's leaders railed against the supercilious Aryan doctrine of the Nazis, but the

American Red Cross separated the blood of blacks and whites in the blood banks that had been developed largely from the work of a black physician, Charles Drew. They spoke out against the brutal treatment of minorities in Germany, but German prisoners of war in the United States received better treatment than blacks in and out of the armed services.

No Negro who had seen it could ever erase from his mind the sight of these war prisoners enjoying better treatment and more luxury than a Negro American could ever dream of enjoying in his own country. This is what Witter Bynner meant when he wrote in 1944:

> On a train in Texas German prisoners sat
> With white American soldiers, seat by seat,
> While black American soldiers sit apart,
> The white men eating meat, the black men heart.
> Now, with that other war a century done,
> Not the live North but the dead South has won,
> Not yet a riven nation comes awake.
> Whom are we fighting this time, for God's sake?
> Mark well the token of the separate seat,
> It is again ourselves whom we defeat.

More than poets spoke out. In 1943 William H. Hastie resigned as civilian aide to the Secretary of War, giving as his reason "Reactionary policies and discriminatory practices of the Army Air Forces in matters affecting Negroes." Walter White, the secretary of the National Association for the Advancement of Colored People, said in 1944 that the United States was doing her full share in the intensification of the effort to permit no fundamental change in the attitude of white nations toward the colored peoples of the earth. "Every lynching, every coldblooded shooting of a Negro soldier in Louisiana or Mississippi or Georgia, every refusal to abolish segregation in our armed forces, every filibuster against an anti-poll tax or anti-lynching bill, every snarling, sneering reference by a Mississippi Senator like Eastland to 'burr headed niggers' in fulmination against an appropriation for the Fair Employment Practice Committee builds up a debit balance of hatred against America which may cost countless lives of Americans yet unborn."

If America paid no attention to the chorus of protests raised by people like Witter Bynner, William Hastie, and Walter White, it could not ignore similar sentiments when expressed in 1947 by President Truman's Committee on Civil Rights. In staccato phrases, it laid down a serious indictment against the nation's racial policies: "We are convinced . . . that the incidence of police brutality against Negroes is disturbingly high. . . . The denial of the suffrage on account of race is the most serious present interference with the right to vote. . . . Discrimination is most acutely felt by minority group members in their inability to get a job suited to their qualifications. . . . If he can get himself hired, the minority worker often finds that he is being paid less than other workers. . . . labor unions are guilty of discriminatory labor practices. . . . The national government should assume leadership in our American civil rights program because there is much in the field of civil rights that it is squarely responsible for in its own direct dealings with millions of persons."

Never before had an agency of the national government spoken so clearly and so unequivocally for racial equality. And never again would the struggle for racial equality be without some assumption of responsibility on the part of some agency that could speak for all or, at least, most of the American people. It was the symbol of national responsibility that was so important. It could be seen in President Truman's moves to eliminate segregation and discrimination in the armed forces, in employment, and in education. It could be seen in the effort to eliminate the ugly spectacle of segregation in the nation's capital. (Once the federal cafeterias and dining rooms were closed on Friday, there was nowhere that a black American could eat on capitol hill on the weekends in 1950.) It could be seen in the role played by the government, as a friend of the court, in the long and finally successful effort to break down segregation in higher education and in the public schools. How much of this could have been accomplished without the aid of the federal government it is difficult to say. That the role of the federal government was significant in the achievement of a semblance of racial equality in these areas is abundantly clear.

The problem of race has never been far from the center of political activity in the United States. It was surely a factor in the presidential elections in the decade before the Civil War and all during Reconstruction. Even as blacks were disfranchised in the last quarter of the nineteenth century they continued to occupy a central place as whipping boys, scapegoats, and evil influences for Americans who insisted that the elimination of Negroes from politics was the only way to keep American politics free of corruption. As Judge J. J. Chrisman told the Mississippi Constitutional Convention in 1890, only a moral idiot would be willing to perpetuate the practice of stuffing ballot boxes, committing perjury, and engaging in fraud and violence in order to eliminate Negroes from political influence. He proposed a scheme of constitutional disfranchisement; and virtually all of his colleagues agreed.

Even in recent times, and particularly since World War II, as the public sector took cognizance of the problem of race, its political importance increased. Whites opposed to racial equality sought to make political capital out of their position. They did this by creating political arms out of the white citizens councils, the Dixiecrats, and other agents of the white backlash. Meanwhile, blacks who reluctantly settled in the urban ghettoes containing millions of potential voters began to translate their numbers into real political power, thereby creating new fears and new problems for those who sought to keep the blacks politically impotent.

No political party wanted to take notice of the problem of race, but the fear that its rival might do so prompted statements or actions that no leaders really wanted to take seriously. Political platforms that paid lip service to traditional American concepts of equality and fair play were to be forgotten, or at least the platform writers hoped they would be. And each major party seemed to be content if by its pious platitudes it merely neutralized the effects of the other's pious platitudes in the racial sphere. Nowhere was the plain assertion made that blacks were entitled to complete political equality. Rather, there was the hope that they would remain as inferior and as inconsequential in politics as they were in other areas.

One of the remarkable consequences of the effort to keep blacks politically impotent and generally degraded was the initially unnoticed black backlash to white intransigence which inevitably resulted in the erosion of that intransigence. Blacks reacted to the revived Ku Klux Klan, the white citizens councils, and the other terrorist organizations with an equanimity that was somewhat disconcerting to whites. They laughed at the Klan parades as they recognized the swagger of Mr. Jones or the limp of Mr. Smith under their white sheets. And they began quietly but firmly to stand their ground in their demand for greater consideration as American citizens. Equally remarkable were the relatively modest demands that blacks made of white officials. They did not demand public office, but merely fair treatment in the administration of justice and an opportunity to participate in the political process. They did not even demand the same public accommodations.

One wonders what would have happened if blacks who wanted to register and vote in the 1950s had been permitted to do so. It is possible that they would have been more inclined to trust the white candidates for public office, voted for them, and manifested no undue interest in holding public office themselves. That is, of course, mere speculation. One wonders what would have happened if Montgomery whites had met the first demands of Dr. Martin Luther King and his associates—to be permitted to enter the front door of the bus and to sit in seats reserved for whites when those seats were vacant. It was white intransigence that caused black voters to conclude they must vote and must hold public office in order to enjoy the first fruits of equality. It was white intransigence that caused Dr. King and his followers to decide they must have desegregated buses and must have black bus drivers in order to ride in dignity.

One supposes that the whites who were resisting the efforts of blacks to enjoy equality were actually operating from the premise that equality could not be shared. Since they assumed that blacks occupied an inferior position in the social order, they believed that equality could not and, indeed, should not be divided between blacks and whites. To the extent that they believed equality could not be divided they were perhaps correct. To the extent that they believed equality could be arrogated to one segment of society and withheld from another segment, they were woefully mistaken. Equality could be shared, but it could not be divided in a way that some would be more equal than others. For some three hundred years those in power in this country have confronted this problem and for most of that time they have succeeded in achieving the democratically incongruous feat of designating who should be equal and who should not be. Offhand, it reminds one of the paintings of Audubon's birds. They are attractive and even plausible, but some of the postures are anatomically impossible.

The incongruity has always been noted by some Americans, if only in passing. Some of the Founding Fathers noted it, but its solution had no priority on their agenda. The abolitionists were quite aware of it, but emancipation, not equality, was their main preoccupation. Partisan politicians were aware of it, but they were unwilling to run the risk of doing anything about it, lest their adversaries take advantage of their move, even for selfish and sinister reasons. Running through every consideration of the matter was the feeling that somehow this was not central to the survival or even to the progress of the country. Hence, one could not get too excited about it. This was a safe, comfortable position to take until about two decades ago, but it did not last. Indeed, it could not last in the face of a growing awareness on the part of an increasing number of Americans that equality was indivisible. This awareness forced itself upon the American people through a series of developments that were both dramatic and significant.

It was one thing to deal with a few Negro leaders and reach some compromise arrangement with them, or buy them off or seek to discredit them and, failing in these efforts, to engage in combat with them and win. That was essentially the pattern for two centuries and more. It reached its climax in what I choose to call the Booker Washington Syndrome in which whites would deal with one Negro leader and having brought that leader under their control had no further worries or concerns. Although a leader like Martin Luther King was abhorrent to them, they at least could focus on him and try to control him, feeling that he was the key to controlling the entire range of Negro aspirations. The Federal Bureau of Investigation had this perception, and this led to its despicable and thoroughly un-American methods of seeking to discredit Dr. King. It was quite another thing to confront not one leader or a few hundred or even a few thousand blacks whose very size made them vulnerable, but to confront several million angry, impatient, aggressive blacks who were willing to risk everything in the battle to achieve equality.

By the 1950s the movement to achieve equality was no longer an elitist movement directed from the offices of the National Association for the Advancement of Colored People and the National Urban

League, but a mass movement; and the very numbers themselves dramatically changed the character of the movement. It was now the Movement for the Liberation of Black People or it was the Black Revolution. It was a movement that took to the streets in Alabama as well as New York to express the chagrin and outrage that blacks felt at having been denied equality for so long. It had more educated, articulate blacks than any earlier egalitarian movement could boast. There were teachers, physicians, lawyers, clergymen, and businessmen. But it also had enormous numbers of common laborers, maids, artisans, union members, and farmers. This not only provided a greater cross-section of the black population than had ever participated in a drive for equality, but it also presented to the general public a picture of solidarity that was hitherto unknown.

From the time of the founding of the National Association for the Advancement of Colored People in 1909, there had been whites in the movement for equal rights for blacks. Indeed, from the beginning, they had assumed leadership roles. Now, they were present in larger numbers than ever before. Some were leaders of interracial groups, others were leaders of religious or labor groups, while others came representing white organizations—friends of the court, as it were—willing to cast their lot with blacks for the common cause. But there were more than white leaders. There were hundreds of thousands of white followers, volunteering to assist in the struggle for equality. Held in suspicion by numerous blacks, they were frequently confined to yeoman service by those blacks who feared that the motivations and the aspirations of the whites might be different from their own. Indeed, some whites were driven out of the movement by some blacks whose paranoia, born of bitter experience, made it impossible for them to work with whites and trust them.

Some whites were doubtless motivated by fear and self-interest. If the movement got out of control and became violent, they did not want to be among those from whom Negroes felt alienated. There were many others, however, who were deeply moved by the opportunity, at long last, to participate in the realization of the long-deferred dream of equality. Some had even come to feel that equality was indivisible and that their own enjoyment of equal rights was a tenuous arrangement so long as equality was not shared by all. It was entirely conceivable that if the equal rights movement became explosive, an unsympathetic government might take drastic steps to repress it. In doing so, it could well assume the posture of a police state and jeopardize the equal rights even of whites. The example of the absence of freedom in those communities where racial orthodoxy demanded that all whites stand together against all blacks was a frightening spectacle to some. The example of South Africa, as the logical extension of that repression, was there for all to see. What good would equal rights be in a country where apartheid prevailed and where even those who enjoyed a semblance of equal rights were not free even to discuss the matter? It had not quite happened here, but it could happen; and sensitive whites seemed to realize this.

It is indeed interesting to observe how the situation outside the United States affected the course of thought and action at home. Foreign critics were quick to see the inconsistency of the United States in matters of equal rights. They saw how stern this country could be in criticizing the absence of equality in other countries. They also saw how reluctant this country was to take an unequivocal stand in favor of equality in such forums as the United Nations, where the sword could easily cut both ways. They, as well as Americans, saw how American economic policies took precedence over United Nations resolutions favoring economic sanctions against countries where racial equality was non-existent, as in the case of Rhodesia. Some American economists and other protagonists of an American policy of duplicity in international dealings argued that American policy was good for, say, Rhodesia as well as for the United States. But others were convinced there were at least some limits to American cynicism that should be observed.

But some developments abroad encouraged Negro Americans to press harder for equality in the United States. Inspired by the achievement of independence and majority rule by black nations in Africa, their efforts to secure equality for themselves took on renewed vigor and determination. As Talcott Parsons has aptly observed, the emergence into independence of the sub-Saharan nations of Africa has enormously changed the worldwide significance of the American race problem and provided a considerable stimulus to the movement for racial equality in the United States. The hands-off attitude of the United States toward liberation movements in Africa unless and until some potential enemy of the United States took a hand in the movement convinced many Negro Americans as well as foreign observers that American foreign policy in Africa too closely resembled the traditional domestic policy in the racial sphere.

Few developments have affected the movement for racial equality more than the assumption of some responsibility by government itself. Within a decade after the Truman Committee on Civil Rights had completed its task, Congress had created the United States Commission on Civil Rights. The significance of the commission lay not so much in the exercise of its quite limited powers or the success of its quite modest program as in its symbolizing a remarkable and historic reversal of congressional policy on matters directly affecting race. And having taken this first, halting step, Congress, responding to pressures from the outside as well as from within, took additional steps. It extended the life of the Commission on Civil Rights and enlarged its powers. A few years later, in 1964, it enacted into law the most far-reaching civil rights bill ever passed by that body, authorizing agents of the government to protect citizens against discrimination in voting, education, and the use of public accommodations. In the following year it passed the Voting Rights Act, which led to a dramatic increase in the number of black voters and ultimately of black elected public officials. Now that the barrier was breached, there would be other legislation in the area, but none as far-reaching or significant as the acts of 1964 and 1965.

The momentum that President Truman initiated in the executive branch continued in later administrations, even when the White House itself was not in the forefront. The Department of Justice busied itself with instituting suits against persons and groups that sought to obstruct the voting process, and it entered litigations as friends of the court when private persons sought relief from racial discrimination. Meanwhile, other departments began to examine their racial policies in the light of increasing pressures to effect changes, while some presidents took steps to end inequality. President Kennedy, by executive order, ended racial discrimination in federally supported housing and established the Committee on Equal Employment Opportunity. President Johnson urged the passage of the Civil Rights Act of 1964 and the Voting Rights Act of 1965; and he greatly enlarged the role of the federal government in extending equality to all citizens. He pledged himself to fight the battle for racial equality "where it should be fought—in the courts, in the Congress, and in the hearts of men."

The courts, moreover, were responsive to the

cases brought before them by persons aggrieved over racial discrimination and to the positions taken by the Department of Justice in support of such persons. In cases involving education, housing, transportation, civil rights, and voting, the federal judiciary handed down a series of landmark decisions during the last three decades that greatly encouraged Negro Americans and all Americans who sought racial equality. In instances where there was stubborn resistance, the courts undertook to supervise the implementation of their own decisions, including the establishment of criteria by which to judge the performance of officials charged with carrying out the judicial mandates.

There was criticism of the courts not only for their decisions but also for their assumption of responsibility in implementation. Strictures against the judiciary were not confined to the segregationists. Distinguished constitutional lawyers and political scientists were dismayed by the intrusion of the judiciary into the details of the administration of justice and into areas best handled, they insisted, by congressional legislation and executive implementation. They did not seem to be disturbed that little had been done by those other branches of government to provide relief to those persons whose constitutional rights had been denied them for generations. Nor did they seem to be distressed that since the decision in *Brown* v. *Board of Education* a generation of blacks had been born and grown to maturity without the equal protection of the laws that the courts sought to give. Had the courts remained silent, the situation would have been infinitely worse. Despite the criticisms the courts held firm to the view that the equal protection of the laws was too precious a part of the United States Constitution to permit it to be frustrated by whim, indifference, or opposition.

For three centuries the people of this country have been greatly absorbed with questions related in one way or another to racial equality. The preoccupation has been obsessive, and the costs have been incalculable. Of course the institution of slavery was profitable, but the damage to the national purpose and even to the national character could not be determined by the plantation bookkeeper. After emancipation the cost was not calculated in terms of slavery, of course, but in terms of segregation, discrimination, and other matters in which race was overriding and frequently took precedence over other considerations.

A few years ago it was estimated that the overall cost of racial discrimination was roughly $17.3 billion or 3.2 per cent of the gross national product. This cost resulted primarily from the failure to utilize fully the existing experience and skills of the total population and the failure to develop fully the potential experience and skills of all persons, particularly blacks. Even in the best of times, such as in the prosperous year of 1964, the unemployment rate for blacks was 9.6 per cent as against 4.6 per cent among whites. In times not quite so good, as in 1975—before the recession had bottomed out—it was estimated that the unemployment rate for blacks was 13.7 per cent as compared to 7.6 for whites.

The effect of this discrimination against black Americans could be seen in their inability to secure employment commensurate with their competence or adequate housing even when it was available or opportunities to rear and educate their children in a wholesome environment or a chance to participate more fully and responsibly in the economic and social life of the country.

Such obviously staggering costs were minor when compared with other more subtle, more insidious costs that could not be translated into dollars and percentages. What did it cost Florida and North Carolina legislators, in the way they viewed themselves and life in general, to enact bills to segregate textbooks used by white children from those used by black children, despite stringent rules covering the fumigation of used textbooks? What possessed the lawmakers of Virginia to undertake twice in this century to define Negroes and whites in terms of the amount of white or Negro blood that coursed through their veins? What did it do to the intellectual climate of a country where people fretted over how much a person's success or failure depended on whether he was nearly white or nearly black? What did it do to the intellectual well-being and the moral health for the president of the University of Kentucky, in his efforts to keep blacks out of the university, to testify in court that his history faculty of twenty-five professors was not superior to the faculty of three at the Negro state college? It is virtually impossible to assess the costs in terms of time, energy, and anxiety that are daily expended in order to maintain what the President's Commission on Civil Disorders described as "two societies, one black, one white—separate and unequal." Small wonder that once, in a moment of sheer exasperation, the distinguished white Southerner Walter Hines Pages said, "The Negro-in-America is a form of insanity that overtakes white men."

It is difficult to imagine or to assess what the experience of three centuries of inequality has done to Negro Americans. In the eighteenth century they witnessed the shaping of a revolutionary doctrine of equality that was deliberately and systematically denied to them even as they fought to secure it for all Americans. Blacks who were free discovered that an uncompromising prerequisite for the enjoyment of equality was to be white; and they could not escape the conclusion that equality based on race was not only strange but also false. In the nineteenth century they witnessed the agonizing justification of inequality on the basis of doctrines of racial inferiority that were as widely accepted as they were bizarre. The characterization of blacks by serious scholars and scientists as stupid, irresponsible, and incapable of maturity dogged them even after emancipation; and their segregation, discrimination, and general degradation were enough to create a sense of helplessness and hopelessness even among the most san-guine.

In the twentieth century they participated in two world wars against the twin evils of totalitarianism and racism. They returned home to riots, burnings alive while still in the uniform of their country, lynchings, and a stubborn, violent resistance to every effort to enjoy the equal protection of the laws. They sought work and housing in the cities but received scarcely a pittance. They reached out for assistance from the more powerful and affluent elements who abandoned them to grope and falter in the decaying inner city. And even when some whites extended a gracious, helping hand, others resisted their quest for equality with a bitter determination and a resourcefulness which all but nullified that quest. The despair born of such conditions reflected itself in the indifference, moral lassitude, pessimism, violence of one against the other, and general debility among persons as well as institutions. If they needed a personal and group reorientation, as indeed they did, they also needed the support of those decision makers and policy makers who had done so much to bring about their tragic plight in the first place.

More than anything else, however, Americans of every race, creed, economic rank, and social position need to recognize that equality is indeed indivisible. For the entire life of this nation an effort has been made to divide equality—to create a social order in which equality was to be enjoyed by some on the basis of race and denied to others because they did not belong to that race—and it has not worked. On the basis of our experience we are now faced with the grim choice of declaring that we shall adhere to a position that equality has no place in our society and sink into a state of general degradation characteristic of other decaying societies or concede that equality is a principle so essential to the shaping of our future and the future of any civilized community that we must abandon the futile policy of seeking to divide it and adhere to the principle of sharing it.

> Then speed the day and haste the hour,
> Break down the barriers, gain the power
> To use the land and sail the sea,
> To hold the tools, unchecked and free;
> No tribute pay, but service give,
> Let each man work that all may live.
> Banish all bonds and usury,
> Be free! Set free!
> Democracy! Democracy!

focused on equality for whites no matter what class but not for blacks.

For Further Reading

The sources cited below are not intended to be either a bibliography on which the 1976 Jefferson Lecture is based or a survey of the works on the history of the struggle for racial equality in America. Rather, they merely suggest some first steps for readers who are interested in exploring further the issues with which the lecture deals. In my *From Slavery to Freedom: A History of Negro Americans* (4th edition, New York, 1974) I have traced the issues in some detail and have included a fairly comprehensive bibliography. The most comprehensive bibliography, however, is James McPherson and others, *Blacks in America: Bibliographical Essays* (Garden City, 1971) in which the reader can find lists of works that deal with every aspect of racial equality. General works that can be read with profit are Kenneth Clark and Talcott Parsons, *The Negro American* (Boston, 1966); Nathan Huggins and others, *Key Issues in the Afro-American Experience*, two volumes (New York, 1971); and August Meier and Elliott Rudwick, *The Making of Black America*, two volumes (New York, 1969).

The authoritative work on Negro Americans and

the problem of equality during the revolutionary era is Benjamin Quarles, *The Negro in the American Revolution* (Chapel Hill, 1966), but one should also consult David Brion Davis, *The Problem of Slavery in the Age of Revolution, 1770–1823* (Ithaca, 1975); Winthrop Jordan, *White over Black: American Attitudes toward the Negro, 1550–1812* (Chapel Hill, 1968); and Arthur Zilbersmit, *The First Emancipation: The Abolition of Slavery in the North* (Chicago, 1967). For Thomas Jefferson's views on race see his *Notes on the State of Virginia* (Paris, 1784), but this should be supplemented by Daniel J. Boorstin, *The Lost World of Thomas Jefferson* (New York, 1948); David Brion Davis, *Was Thomas Jefferson an Authentic Enemy of Slavery?* (Oxford, 1970); Robert McColley, *Slavery and Jeffersonian Virginia;* and William Cohen, "Thomas Jefferson and the Problem of Slavery," *Journal of American History* 56 (December 1968): 503–26.

The manner in which racial attitudes of white Americans became established in law and public policy may be approached in a variety of ways. Among the works that will be helpful in such an undertaking are Donald Robinson, *Slavery in the Structure of American Politics, 1765–1820* (New York, 1971); William Stanton, *Scientific Attitudes toward Race in America, 1815–1859* (Chicago, 1960); and George M. Frederickson, *The Black Image in the White Mind: The Debate on Afro-American Character and Destiny, 1817–1914* (New York, 1971). The experience of whites with free blacks, which had a permanent effect on their attitudes, is discussed in Leon Litwack, *North of Slavery: The Negro in the Free States, 1790–1860* (Chicago, 1961), and Ira Berlin, *Slaves without Masters: The Free Negro in the Antebellum South* (New York, 1974).

I have dealt with the problems of equality in the years following the Civil War in *Reconstruction after the Civil War* (Chicago, 1961). C. Vann Woodward has treated the matter in several significant essays, "Equality: The Deferred Commitment" and "The Political Legacy of Reconstruction" in his *The Burden of Southern History* (Baton Rouge, 1960) and in his *The Strange Career of Jim Crow* (3d revised edition, New York, 1974). James McPherson has analyzed several aspects of the problem in *The Struggle for Equality: Abolitionists and the Negro in the Civil War and Reconstruction* (Princeton, 1964). See also Forrest G. Wood, *The Black Scare: The Racist Response to Emancipation and Reconstruction* (Berkeley, 1969).

The authoritative work on the decline of racial equality in the post-Reconstruction years is Rayford Logan, *The Negro in American Life and Thought: The Nadir, 1877–1901* (New York, 1954), revised and reissued in 1965 as *The Betrayal of the Negro: From Rutherford B. Hayes to Woodrow Wilson*. Idus A. Newby's *Jim Crow's Defense: Anti-Negro Thought in America, 1900–1930* (Baton Rouge, 1965) and Thomas Dixon's novel, *The Leopard's Spots: A Romance of the White Man's Burden* (New

111

York, 1902) indicate in different ways some major obstacles to racial equality. The role of the federal judiciary is treated in Loren Miller, *The Petitioners: The Story of the Supreme Court of the United States and the Negro* (New York, 1966).

The essays by W. E. B. Du Bois in *Souls of Black Folk* (Chicago, 1903) and his *Dusk of Dawn: An Essay toward an Autobiography of a Race Concept* (New York, 1940) provide a setting for understanding the problem in the early years of this century. Booker Washington's role is discussed in Louis R. Harlan, "The Secret Life of Booker T. Washington," *Journal of Southern History* 37 (August 1971): 393–416. The role of the black press is evaluated in the careers of three leading editors in Roi Ottley, *The Lonely Warrior: The Life and Times of Robert S. Abbott* (Chicago, 1955); Emma Lou Thornbrough, *T. Thomas Fortune: Militant Journalist* (Chicago, 1972); and Stephen R. Fox, *The Guardian of Boston: William Monroe Trotter* (New York, 1970). The attitudes of the Presidents are discussed in George Sinkler, *The Racial Attitudes of American Presidents* (Garden City, 1971); Arthur S. Link, *The New Freedom* (Princeton, 1956); and Nancy Weiss, "The Negro and the New Freedom: Fighting Wilsonian Segregation," *Political Science Quarterly* 84 (March 1969): 61–79. The role of the NAACP and the National Urban League can be followed in Charles Flint Kellogg, *NAACP: A History of the National Association for the Advancement of Colored People* (Baltimore, 1967), and Nancy J. Weiss, *The National Urban League, 1910–1940* (New York, 1974).

The literature on racial equality in recent years is enormous. Among the outstanding works concerning government's role are *To Secure These Rights: The Report of the President's Committee on Civil Rights* (New York, 1947); the annual *Report of the United States Commission on Civil Rights* (Washington, 1958–) and frequent interim reports; and the *Report of the National Advisory Commission on Civil Disorders* (New York, 1968). General studies include Richard Bardolph, *The Civil Rights Record: Black Americans and the Law, 1849–1970* (New York, 1970); Henry S. Commager, *The Struggle for Equality: A Documentary Record* (New York, 1967); and Albert P. Blaustein and Robert L. Zangrando, *Civil Rights and the American Negro: A Documentary History* (New York, 1968).

One should not overlook the writings of Martin Luther King, Jr., one of which is *Why We Can't Wait* (New York, 1964); Whitney Young, Jr., *To Be Equal* (New York, 1964); Kenneth Clark, *Dark Ghetto: Dilemmas of Social Power* (New York, 1965); Eldridge Cleaver, *Soul on Ice* (New York, 1968); James Boggs, *The American Revolution: Pages from a Negro Worker's Notebook* (New York, 1963); and Frank Hercules, *American Society and Black Revolution* (New York, 1972).